On the Way to Fun

On the Way to Fun

An Emotion-Based Approach to Successful Game Design

Roberto Dillon
DigiPen Institute of Technology

A K Peters, Ltd.
Natick, Massachusetts

Editorial, Sales, and Customer Service Office

A K Peters, Ltd.
5 Commonwealth Road
Natick, MA 01760
www.akpeters.com

Library of Congress Cataloging-in-Publication Data

Dillon, Roberto.
  On the way to fun : an emotion-based approach to successful game design / Roberto Dillon.
      p. cm.
  Includes bibliographical references and index.
  ISBN 978-1-56881-582-4 (alk. paper)
  1. Computer games—Programming. 2. Computer games—Design—Social aspects. I. Title.
  QA76.76.C672D54 2919
  794.8'1526—dc22
          2009050148

Cover image © Veer Incorporated.

Printed in the United States of America
14 13 12 11 10   10 9 8 7 6 5 4 3 2 1

To Jing

Table of Contents

117   Case Studies: Indie Games

155   Conclusions

165   References

167   Index

Foreword

Have you ever felt really happy and joyful or really angry because of playing a video game? How often do you experience those deeply emotional moments in games? I remember quite vividly when I angrily punched my Game Boy's screen while playing *Double Dragon*, cracking the screen, and how happy I was when I finally beat the boss that gave me so much trouble. I remember my amazement during the opening of *Half-Life* and when I couldn't stop laughing as I clicked my way through *Monkey Island*. And the several occasions of breaking into tears playing *Shadow of the Colossus* are following me around to this day. But despite all the games I have played, there are less than a handful that I still remember vividly, if at all.

When I started to get interested in game design and able to analyze games properly, I quickly realized that what most differentiates games from any other medium is not their interactivity, but their lack of emotional impact. The fact that you would really care about a game character or the game world was, for most games, not a priority.

When I had the opportunity at the beginning of my career to join Lionhead Studios to work on *Black & White* and learn about game design from Peter Molyneux, it became quite clear why he was hailed one of the geniuses of the industry. Almost a year after my short stint in the UK, I fortuitously met Shigeru Miyamoto and was able to probe his brain for a bit. I learned that he has a very similar thought about games—the player needs to get attached to something in the game world and really care about it. Then the player experiences the game hand-in-hand with this object of attachment and thus the game creates emotional moments. This notion is not limited to story-driven games. Any game can and should create those moments. Some are very easy to create, but the ones with most impact are tough. I made it a rule from then on that everything I design must consider the emotional reaction of the user. That premise should be applied to any kind of design, not just games.

During the past year, I worked closely with Roberto on the Music and Emotion Driven Game Engine (M-EDGE) research project, and finally had the opportunity to incorporate emotion into games in a way almost unheard of before. Roberto helped me to design a game that could, like a living being, have a real emotional reaction to music, and have an impact on the game world as well as the player. It sure did change our moods very quickly at times.

Roberto's expertise in music and his experience with emotional systems became very quickly a valuable resource for me. He is someone who, with his dedication, critical thinking, and decisiveness brought out the best in our endeavor of creating a game with emotional consideration and impact. Both of us have had the good fortune to experience the world in many ways and his openness to new ideas helped me progress in my own field.

Roberto is an excellent researcher who is looking at the advancement of game development through new and sometimes unusual means, and who doesn't take things for granted. I wish many of the points raised here by Roberto had been as explicitly written out much earlier—maybe I wouldn't have broken my Game Boy in the first place. I hope this book will become a very valuable tool for you too.

Simon Rozner
Singapore
August 12, 2009

Preface

I spent the last few weeks commuting to and from work on the bus while carefully studying *The Art of Computer Game Design* by Chris Crawford [Crawford 84]. Needless to say, I enjoyed that pioneering book tremendously, not only for the actual contents, which are still mostly valid and able to make us really *think* about game design, but also for Crawford's concision and synthesis skills. In just about 80 pages, he could clearly explain his ideas. Crawford's book was the first one dedicated to videogame design. Countless more followed and today game design books are getting extremely comprehensive, insightful, and…massive.

This is obviously very exciting for all of us who have an interest in games, whether as a profession or as a hobby. But for those who, like me, keep trying to squeeze reading and studying into our busy daily work schedules, reading a 1000+ page tome on a crowded bus or subway train isn't an easy task at all! This was one of my concerns when I started writing this little book. I wanted to be as concise and focused as possible and deliver my message in a small, agile book that could easily be carried around and read anywhere whenever there are five minutes free.

With respect to the actual contents, my objective was to provide some food for thought by clarifying which emotions and instincts are particularly relevant within the gaming medium and how they can interact with each other to enhance the gaming experience. This can hopefully help us with the oldest design problem of all—how to make a "fun" game—by giving us a fresh perspective on how to properly design and develop gameplay ideas in a way that makes these interactions straightforward and natural.

In doing this, I wanted to recall some old and fond memories in those who, like me, are old enough to have witnessed the beginning of our industry. I also hoped to excite some curiosity among the new generations by analyzing several case studies coming from the so-called "retro gaming" scene, in particular by focusing on those games that were published between the late seventies and mid-eighties.

Overall, this book was written for aspiring and beginning game designers who want to know a little more about human nature, emotions, and instincts and their important place in designing games. I am also confident that, by formalizing concepts in a simple and straightforward way that were usually left to academic studies, the book may even be of some help to more experienced professionals by making them aware of something they may well have already used, but only at a subconscious level thanks to their own personal intuition and skills.

Roberto Dillon
Singapore
July 4, 2009

Introduction: What Makes a Game Fun?

> Art is something designed to evoke emotion through
> fantasy…The computer game is an art form because
> it presents its audience with fantasy experiences that
> stimulate emotion.
>
> —Chris Crawford
> *The Art of Computer Game Design*

What makes a game fun? And what is "fun" actually? Unfortunately
providing an exhaustive and objective answer to these legitimate
questions is likely to be an impossible task since having fun is
a very personal activity that can be completely different from
individual to individual.

In fact, what is fun for someone can be extremely boring
for somebody else and vice versa. For example, some people find
watching a football match to be an extremely fun and exhilarating activity, while others would definitely skip it and spend their
free time doing something else. Videogames are no exception,
and even within them there are many subcategories that attract
and provide fun experiences to only a specific group of people.
So the aim of this small book is not to try to directly answer
"what makes a game fun" but rather to provide a simple and easy
to understand framework that links successful yet simple games
to basic human emotions and instincts.

Why? Well, the idea is to show aspiring and beginning game
designers how certain games successfully relied on behavioral
aspects deeply rooted in human beings to provide experiences
that completely immersed players in those experiences. In doing
this, we are assuming that such games were able to deliver a truly

entertaining experience and we will analyze the reasons why the games were so engaging that they were ultimately perceived as fun—however we define this concept.

The book is structured in different parts. The first part provides a theoretical framework for analyzing gameplay in terms of underlying emotions. The proposed model is called the "6-11 Framework" after the 6 basic emotions and 11 instincts it takes into consideration. In particular, after a quick introduction to basic emotions and instincts, we discuss which ones are more relevant in videogames and how they can be used to affect and influence players' experiences. To do this, we will define a "path", or "way", that, by having different emotions and instincts as intermediate stops, will likely lead us to the final destination of "fun".

The remaining parts are dedicated to a collection of case studies with a special focus on old retro games. In Part II, we will review and analyze a selection of 20 meaningful examples from the 1970s and 1980s to show how, by basing their gameplay on a few of the emotions and instincts considered in the 6-11 Framework, they succeeded in engaging generations of players despite being developed with very limited technical means and without any fancy graphics or realistic sounds. Alongside these, we discuss a couple of games that didn't live up to their expectations. This will be instructive and also a little provocative as we will try to explain the reasons for their partial or complete failure by pointing out how they overlooked or misinterpreted some particular emotion or instinct which resulted in the players feeling less engaged and immersed in the overall gaming experience. In Part III we will look at how the proposed framework could be applied to more contemporary productions by analyzing a few well-known modern independent ("indie") games. Finally, Part IV will conclude with some thoughts about the broader picture of the usefulness of our approach.

PART I

Emotions and Games: The 6-11 Framework

*Defining Emotions and Instincts and How They Can
Lead the Way to Fun in Videogames*

What Are Basic Emotions and Instincts?

We started our introduction by saying that defining "fun" is an impossible task due to its inherently subjective nature, so we turned our attention to the understanding of basic emotions, hoping that they will help us in discovering an alternative path still leading the way toward fun in games. While very useful, this framework carries some limitations. Even though the study of emotions has received considerable attention in the scientific and psychological communities within the last 100 years, there does not appear to be definitive agreement on their nature or which ones, if any, are considered "basic", or fundamental.

Some researchers categorized only two emotions as basic—happiness and sadness [Weiner and Graham 84]. Other researchers cite as many as ten or more (e.g., anger, contempt, disgust, distress, fear, guilt, interest, joy, shame, surprise) [Izard 77]. Some related basic emotions to unique facial expressions [Ekman 99] and [Ekman 04], while others followed different cues and approaches. In any case, most lists usually include emotions such as happiness, sadness, anger, and fear (or their respective synonyms) and these are often considered hardwired in the brain through means of the natural evolution of the species (see, e.g., [Plutchik 82]).

Despite the disagreement on which emotions are considered basic, it's important to note that most researchers still tend to believe in a core, more primordial, set of emotions. From these core emotions all other innumerable ones can be derived by following different theories and approaches, often in a way similar to the derivation of any color from a set of three fundamental ones.

These basic emotions, in turn, can relate to basic instincts in different ways. But before analyzing their interactions, we should also specify what we mean by "instincts". In fact, even the analysis of instincts can spur disagreement among sociologists and psychologists, with some even denying that humans now have any instincts at all! This apparently surprising conclusion derives from the notion that our culture and civilization allow us to override or control them [Robertson 89]. Here are the generally accepted characteristics of instincts.

(a) They are automatic.
(b) They are irresistible.
(c) They occur at some point in development.
(d) They are triggered by some event in the environment.
(e) They occur in every member of the species.
(f) They cannot be modified.
(g) They govern a behavior for which the organism needs no training.

Typical and well-known basic human instincts are, for example,

- survival,
- aggressiveness,
- protection/caring,
- collecting,
- reproduction.

Whether we actually can control our own instincts or not, characteristic (d)—triggered by an event—is the focal one for game designers who must figure out how to trigger and manipulate events to provide new and immersive gaming experiences.

For our purposes, we can simply take the others for granted and let sociologists debate each other over them.

So, how can we trigger a particular instinct? A very good example is a sudden loud noise from a hidden, unknown source. Such an event will excite a strong fear emotion that, in turn, will trigger a corresponding survival instinct. Survival can take the form of fighting against the threat or trying to escape from it, which is also known as the "fight or flight" behavior.

Other times, the relationship between emotions and instincts works in the opposite way. Let's imagine we just found the very rare stamp that we needed to complete our valuable album started many years earlier. This discovery will trigger our collecting instinct that will make us crave as many related items of a particular type as possible. That's why so many people all around the world have the hobby of collecting something. Amazingly, this collecting instinct has been hardwired in our brain since the beginning of human kind! Suppose though, that for some reason we are not able to get the stamp—maybe the owner doesn't want to sell it or the requested price is too high and we cannot afford it. This will ultimately trigger a particular emotion which could be anger, frustration, or sadness, according to our personality and self-control capabilities.

Throughout this book we will see several examples of how different emotions and instincts were effectively triggered by a proper use of different settings, storylines, or in-game events to build new gameplay experiences that were exciting and immersive. Nonetheless it is worth pointing out that all these topics have been hotly debated for decades by highly respected researchers and there remains a lack of agreement about them, including universally accepted definitions. So, I guess now we need to wish ourselves good luck in this critical endeavor and hope that our straightforward analysis will still allow us to get a better understanding of how, and why, games are so much…fun!

Introducing the 6-11 Framework

As discussed in the previous section, there is no general agreement on which, among all possible emotions and instincts, are the basic ones. However, we can still try to identify a small subset that seems to be more suitable to be correlated with our medium. In particular, we will be using a framework based on only 6 emotions, 11 instincts, and their interactions—the 6-11 Framework.

These are the six emotions on which we will focus our analysis.

Fear. This is one of the most common emotions in games today. In fact, thanks to the newest technologies, it is very easy to represent realistic environments and situations where fear can be triggered—dim the lights, place the player in a confined space with dark corners and hidden spots, and make a creature suddenly shout right behind the player…et voilà! We only need think of all of the recent survival horror games or dungeon explorations in role playing games (RPG) for plenty of modern examples.

Anger. Anger is a powerful emotion often used as a motivational factor to play again (e.g., if the player gets defeated by some challenging opponent) or to advance in the story to correct any wrongs inflicted by some bad guy.

Joy/happiness. Joy is the most common emotion associated with games and, arguably, one of the most relevant for having a fun gaming experience. Usually this is a consequence of the player succeeding in some task and being rewarded by means of power-ups, story advancements, and so on.

Pride. Often pride will kick in once the game is over as a consequence of a high score with related bragging rights to show off the successful performance to friends and other players. Pride can also be used as a motivational factor in pushing players to improve themselves and advance in the game further by providing rewards or even more difficult challenges. For example, players should feel they are good enough to beat that obnoxious final boss or smart enough to solve that mind-bending puzzle and will try hard to improve their skills to succeed. Particular care needs to be considered here, though—if the challenge is too tough, pride can turn into frustration and players may drop the game altogether. So, when trying to rely on pride to keep players interested in the game through means of difficult challenges, it must be carefully fine-tuned and tested.

Sadness. This emotion is probably the most difficult one to achieve because obviously sadness doesn't really seem to correspond to fun. Nonetheless, game designers have always been attracted by sadness as they aspired to bring their creations to new artistic heights by making games able to touch more complex and mature themes. This requires an immersive story so that the player can feel a strong bond with the gaming world and different "non-playable characters" (NPC). See the analysis of the game *Planet Fall* in Part II for the first game that successfully achieved this.

Excitement. This is the final result most games worth playing should achieve, as it is most likely the closest we can get to our ultimate objective of fun. It should happen naturally as a consequence of successfully triggering other emotions and/or instincts. Many different ways of bringing excitement to the overall experience are possible. For example, putting players under time pressure to accomplishing a particular task or mission, or changing the pace of the game can also be quite effective. These events will likely result in a more hectic experience that will make the player feel more excited and involved in the action.

Now let's now turn our attention to the basic instincts and behaviors that seem to be heavily involved in games. For this purpose, it is useful to group them into three main categories.

- ⬎ *First person* instincts are those that are directed toward ourselves and are for our own preservation and well-being.
- ⬎ *Third person* instincts are directed toward others. This group includes contrasting instincts, showing both our good and evil sides that sometimes drive us to help people in need while at other times drive us to take advantage of them.
- ⬎ *World* instincts are directed toward the interaction with surrounding environments.

In particular, we will concentrate on the following 11 instincts:

First Person

Survival (fight or flight). The most fundamental and primordial of all instincts, triggered when we, like any other living being, are faced with a life threat. According to the situation, our brain will instantly decide whether we should face the threat and fight for our life or try to avoid it by finding a possible way of escaping.

Self-identification. People tend to admire successful individuals or smart fictional characters and naturally start to imagine being like their models. All kids dream to replicate the feats of their heroes and wish they could be like them—whether they have superhuman powers like Superman or Harry Potter, or they are tough guys like Duke Nukem in the famous *3D Realms* games or even average but lovable guys like Guybrush Threepwood in the classic LucasArts game *Secrets of Monkey Island*. It doesn't really matter as long as the games succeed in exciting the fantasy of their fans.

Collecting. As discussed in a previous example, collecting something can be a very strong instinct that can link to a variety of different emotions and it has always been widely used in games. Whether we are talking about the dots in games as old as *Pac-Man* or all the possible achievements in one of the latest Xbox Live Arcade (XBLA) games, the underlying principle is the same—they all rely on this powerful instinct.

Greed. Often we are also prone to go beyond a simple collection and start wishing to amass as many things as possible. Whether they are valuable items or just goods and resources we need to build our virtual empire in a strategy game, a greedy instinct is likely to surface very early in our gaming habits.

Third Person

Protection/care/nurture. Arguably the best instincts of all—the ones that push all parents to love their children and every person to feel the impulse for caring and helping those in need. Many successful games have been designed to resonate with these instincts alone, like the widely popular *Nintendogs* series by Nintendo on their DS console.

Aggressiveness. The other side of the coin, usually leading to violence when coupled with greed or anger. It is exploited in countless games.

Revenge. Another powerful instinct that can act as a motivational force and is often used in games to advance the storyline or justify why we need to annihilate some "bad guy."

Competition. Deeply linked with the social aspects of our psyche and one of the most important instincts in games. Without it, games would lose much of their appeal. In fact, we tend to be always ready to compete with others and this can be easily associated with other instincts and needs such as

- ⬎ Proving ourselves and being acknowledged by others for our results, and
- ⬎ Socializing and interacting with other people—something that designers of massively multiplayer online (MMO) games have obviously understood very well!

Communication. The need for expressing ideas, thoughts, or just gossip was one of the most influential for human evolution and it can be used to great effect in games too, whether in relating with NPCs or other players (e.g. chat rooms in MMO games).

World

Curiosity. All human discoveries, whether of a scientific or geographical nature, have been made thanks to this instinct that always pushes us toward the unknown. And also pushes many gamers to get into that spooky manor at the end of the road without knowing who, or what, may be lurking behind its closed doors....

Color appreciation. We are naturally attracted by colorful scenes and environments, something that undoubtedly influenced our artistic sides, including the appreciation for increasingly detailed and colorful graphics in games.

Having identified the instincts and emotions of interest, we should analyze how they can interact. In general, there can be many different ways for them to correspond to and enhance each other but, in our context, let's narrow our scope and focus only on a subset of possible main relationships and correspondences, as shown in the Figure 1.

EMOTIONS   INSTINCTS

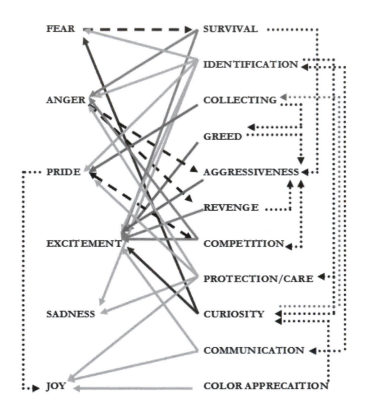

Figure 1. Possible main relationships between basic emotions and instincts. Solid lines indicate instincts to emotions; dashed lines, from emotions to instincts; dotted lines indicate interactions within the same group.

The underlying idea is that fun can be achieved by stimulating different emotions in series or in parallel. This will then form a sequence that, through a corresponding set of game dynamics which are sought after by the player once the proper basic instincts have been triggered, usually ends with excitement and/or joy. This network of relationships makes the backbone of the 6-11 Framework that we will be using to analyze different games and find out how they successfully exploited players' emotions.

To get a better understanding, let's have a closer look at the picture by analyzing the interactions between each emotion and instinct one by one.

Instincts

Survival. Whether we try to escape or we decide to face the danger and fight, the adrenaline rush triggered by the survival instinct will provide new *excitement* to the gaming experience. The survival instinct can also lead to *aggressiveness* and, once the threat is over, it may lead to the instinct of *revenge* through *anger*.

Identification. If the game succeeds in making us identify with an in-game virtual character (or avatar), all possible emotions will be easier to achieve. In general, a proper character identification will likely bring more *excitement* for the upcoming adventures and we will be immersed in the game and feel more *proud* of our virtual successes or *sad* and disappointed for any eventual failure. It will also make players more involved and immersed in the story and virtual world, enhancing their *curiosity* of exploring it and willingness to know more about it. It can also lead to *protection/care* for in-game characters or for the player's avatar itself.

Collecting. This will make players *proud* of their achievements and can also easily lead to *greed* and push them to want more and more. *Collecting* can eventually be reached through *curiosity* due to some findings in a successful exploration.

Greed. It can be reached through *collecting* and it can also turn straight into *excitement* (for example, while gambling) or make us more *aggressive* to satisfy our wishes.

Aggressiveness. It can be triggered by *survival* and *greed* instincts and it can make us look for further challenges and *competition*. The ensuing conflicts can, in turn, make us more aggressive. Different emotions can easily lead to aggressiveness, most importantly *anger* and *fear*.

Competition. This can happen both within the game itself and outside of it (within the player's communities and social circle of friends). Competition will naturally lead to *excitement* and eventually to *anger* in case of defeat, or *pride* in case of success. It can also interact both ways with *aggressiveness* and be triggered by the wish for *revenge*.

Revenge. It can be triggered by *anger* due to a failure and can drive to *aggressiveness*, eventually leading to *competition*, for example to have another chance. And planning and executing revenge can lead straight to *excitement*.

Protection/care. According to the result of the interactions with the object of our care, these instincts can lead to *joy*, for example if we save someone we care about, *pride*, or even *sadness* in case of a loss. It can be reached through a strong immersion within the game, possibly from the *identification* instinct. It can also lead to *anger* and be a motivational factor to justify *aggressiveness* if the object of our care is threatened by something or someone.

Curiosity. Exploring the world and getting more in depth into the story can lead to *excitement* or even *fear*, if the player is led toward dangers. It can also lead us to discover something interesting, triggering the *collecting* instinct. Like protection, curiosity can be enhanced by strong immersion and i*dentification* and also by *color appreciation* as players will feel attracted by areas particularly beautiful and colorful.

Color appreciation. This can lead to *curiosity* or directly to *joy*. It is not by chance that so many players consider beautiful graphics a very important aspect of their enjoyment of their gaming experiences.

Communication. Communicating with NPCs, other players, or even with the system itself can bring *excitement* and *joy*, in addition to helping to immerse the player in the game and contributing to set up the proper *identification*.

Emotions

Fear. One of the most commonly used emotions in games. It can be triggered by *curiosity* and will naturally lead to the *survival* instinct and eventually to *aggressiveness*. Fear is easier to achieve if a proper *identification* with the in-game character is first established.

Anger. It can trigger *revenge* or *aggressiveness* and can be raised by a strong *competitive* mood, a *competition* gone wrong, or a threat/attack we *survived*, as long as a proper *identification* is achieved first.

Joy (or happiness). One of the emotions most closely related to fun. Joy is often reached through *pride* but it can also be triggered through other means like a smart design of the aesthetics of the virtual world (i.e., through *color appreciation)*, by rewarding the player at the right times (e.g., offering cut scenes or bonus stages after beating a level), or by designing amusing interactions between the player and a NPC (*communication*).

Pride. Most successful endeavors will make the player feel proud of his achievements and can involve *identification, collecting, competition,* and *protection/care*, leading to *joy* and *happiness*. On the other hand, pride can also lead to *aggressiveness* through *competition* if we feel that our honor/abilities are being questioned.

Sadness. It will usually enter the picture when something related to *identification* or *protection/care* goes wrong. In its simplest form it may just mean that the player is sad for having lost a game, but it can be much more meaningful and emotionally intense if strictly related to the game's story itself (e.g., a loss that can not be avoided even when successful).

Excitement. Many different sequences can lead to *excitement*, as soon as different emotions capture the player's attention and imagination. *Survival, identification, greed, competition, revenge, curiosity,* and *communication* can all bring new excitement to the player.

All of these different emotions and instincts can surface while playing games and can subconsciously affect the player, involving him or her in an immersive experience that has no equal among other forms of entertainment. Where else can we experience such a broad range of different emotions, including contrasting ones, in just a limited amount of time?

Learning how these different aspects of human psychology can be integrated into games is the skill that makes our medium unique and the work of game designers so fascinating, but also so difficult.

We will need lots of experience and practice to be successful and, to start understanding how all this could actually work in practice, we will see several examples in the second part of this book where we will analyze different games using this particular emotion- and instinct-based framework.

Contextualizing the 6-11 Framework

While the 6-11 Framework can easily be used as a stand-alone tool to analyze particular game experiences, it is surely well worth the effort of contextualizing it among some of the other theoretical models and ideas that have been proposed recently within the game design community to gain a broader picture of the game under scrutiny. Interestingly, it seems often possible to relate and/or integrate our framework within these different approaches and the resulting synergies may offer a slightly new perspective to face old and new problems alike.

Hopefully, the integration and concurrent use of different methodologies like these would provide the attentive designer with new tools to gain an even deeper insight on how emotions can influence and relate to so many varied playing experiences.

The MDA Framework

The MDA Framework, as proposed in [Hunicke, LeBlanc, Zubek 04], is one of the most well-known models to support game designers in their creative process and it has been adopted and popularized by the game design workshops held at the Game Developers Conference since 2001. This model is built upon the concepts of "Mechanics, Dynamics, and Aesthetics" (Figure 2) which have been described and referenced in many different works and publications, including a clear and succinct definition in [Brathwaite and Schreiber 09, page 17] which is worth quoting here to quickly grasp its core elements.

> Aesthetics don't refer to the looks of the game but rather the emotional response the designer and development team

hope to evoke in the players through the game dynamics. If mechanics are the rules and dynamics are the play of the game, then aesthetics are typically the fun (or lack thereof) experienced by playing.

In other words, mechanics are the basic actions by which the game is played while dynamics show what happens as a consequence of applying such actions. Aesthetics, in the end, represent the player's emotional engagement and response while playing.

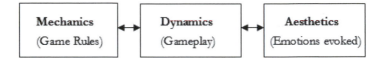

Figure 2. A schematic view of the MDA framework.

For example, a game in which we play a merchant trying to amass vast fortunes will likely have "buying" and "selling" as core game mechanics, resulting in a "trading" dynamic with a corresponding *greed* as the main aesthetic. In this context, the 6-11 Framework appears to be a useful additional tool which can be integrated to gain a further insight into the *aesthetics* of a game, complementing MDA's emotional taxonomy (the "8 Kinds of Fun"). This synergy may then help in relating the emerging emotions and instincts to different game dynamics. Indeed, we will be using a MDA-inspired approach throughout the book.

The "Four Fun Keys"

The "Four Fun Keys" is a framework proposed by Nicole Lazzaro [Lazzaro 09] where player experiences are seen as aiming at different types of fun that are associated with a set of several possible emotions. Following are Lazzaro's four types of fun.

- *Hard Fun.* Players overcome different obstacles within the game. The primary related emotion is "fiero" (from the Italian noun "fierezza" which translates in English as *pride*).
- *Easy Fun.* Players' enjoyment is directly related to experiencing all the different facets and activities offered within the game world. The main related emotion here is *curiosity*.
- *Serious Fun.* These are games that completely capture the players' attention to ultimately change their inner moods and in doing so, succeed in avoiding boredom. The main related emotions are *relaxation* and *excitement*.
- *People Fun.* These are multiplayer events where the social aspect of being together plays a major role in defining the overall experience. The main related emotion is *amusement*.

Interestingly, here the 6-11 Framework maps very nicely to the described four types of fun by offering an alternative set of strategies for reaching them through paths related to a different set of emotions and instincts.

For example, while hard fun is clearly based on a path centered on pride plus its consequent joy and easy fun is based on the instinct of curiosity (note that the Four Fun Keys model does not explicitly distinguish between emotions and instincts and labels everything under the former), things get more unpredictable with serious fun. Here the instinct of identification is of paramount importance for completely immersing the player in the game and then driving him or her toward excitement or a simple and relaxing joy through all possible relations that are underlined within the 6-11 Framework in Figure 1.

Last, people fun can be clearly seen as resulting from a mix of those instincts that can easily be excited within a small group of friends, such as competition, revenge, aggressiveness, and communication. A beautiful example of this type of fun can be found in the game *Spy vs. Spy.*

Emotioneering™

> Emotioneering™ is the vast body of techniques created and/or distilled by David Freeman, which can create, for a player or participant, a breadth and depth of emotions in a game or other interactive experience—or which can immerse a game player or interactive participant in a world or a role.
>
> –David Freeman
> http://www.FreemanGames.com

Three hundred of these techniques, grouped into 32 categories, are described in [Freeman 03], a very interesting collection of ideas and possible strategies to emotionally engage players. By studying Freeman's ideas, we can see how many techniques refer to aspects of emotion or instinct that can be mapped directly to the 6-11 Framework. For example, there are many techniques relating to the identification instinct (to make the player more immersed in the story, e.g., "role induction technique," "first-person deepening technique," etc.), the protection instinct (e.g., "player chemistry toward NPC technique" to create a bond with a NPC), curiosity (by adding new unknown elements through the "motivation technique"), and so on.

The 6-11 Framework can be used here as a way to provide a possible categorization by grouping different techniques according to their underlying instincts and emotions. This approach can allow game designers an alternative way of indexing and searching the proposed set of techniques for determining which are the most suitable in a given circumstance to enhance a particular emotional state.

Emotions Through Character Design

There are many aspects of game design that can play a meaningful role in defining players' emotional experiences, and character design is surely one of the most relevant. The most comprehensive work on the subject is arguably [Isbister 06], which summarizes the author's extensive research and knowledge in this domain. By reading this text we can see how several of the main aspects emphasized by Isbister can actually help in defining the emotional characteristics that are relevant also to the 6-11 Framework. Among other things, we realize how important it is to craft characters that are engaging (helping players' overall immersion) and approachable (which can directly link to the care/protection instinct if needed).

A proper character design is also required to achieve an effective player's identification, which can be obtained through the wise use of visual affordances providing subconscious emotional cues. For example, the use of appropriate faces, voices, and styles can do wonders to help players identify with a given virtual character. Identification obtained through character design can also effectively be used to move the playing experience towards certain specific directions and trigger particular emotions when needed (e.g., if the player has a mean grin, is wearing torn clothes, and is frantically waving a chainsaw, a resulting identification will likely stimulate players' aggressiveness).

Overall, a proper character design can make the implementation of a given emotional path from the 6-11 Framework, like the one exemplified in Figure 3, much easier and more effective. At the same time, the use of the 6-11 Framework can also point us in the right direction by suggesting the proper cues for designing the most suitable characters in a specific emotional set-up.

Emotional Analysis of a Gameplay Session

Now that we have identified which emotions and instincts are particularly relevant in a gaming scenario and likely to affect players, we can try to analyze how games can emotionally involve them into the action. This usually happens in three phases.

First and foremost (Phase 1), the game has to attract the player's attention and stimulate his or her curiosity about it. To achieve this, it has to satisfy the conditions of familiarity and immediateness. These conditions are fundamental to make the player feel at ease in the virtual setting and can usually happen both at a conscious and subconscious level.

Familiarity is achieved by using a well-known theme, like a setting inspired by popular legends, folklore, historical events (for example, World War II, the Roman Empire, science fiction novels, and so on), or even by referencing other popular games so that the player will naturally frame the game within the proper—familiar—context. Note that as it progresses, the game doesn't necessarily have to faithfully adhere to the familiar background that was set at the beginning. In fact, at times, it can just be used as an expedient to make the player comfortable and then switch the action or story/leitmotif toward other, unexpected, directions. We will see an example of something ultimately unfamiliar but still beginning within a familiar context with the game *3D Monster Maze* in Part II.

Immediate means that the player will instinctively find the way to play while also getting a clear idea of what the goal is, even without reading lengthy and complex instructions. This is something that was achieved in early games by using the so called "attract" (or "demo") mode where the game played a small sequence automatically to show prospective players what it was all about and how it should be played. Today, this is usually done by means of smart tutorials that gradually teach players how to use all of the skills and techniques they will need as the game progresses. Once the player feels familiar with the game and knows what to do and how, it is time to start playing. This brings us to Phase 2—the actual gameplay session.

Here is where the 6-11 Framework comes into the picture since we have to rely upon basic instincts and emotions and their relationships and interactions, as seen in the previous section, to provide a worth-playing experience. To achieve this, the game designer has to build different gameplay dynamics trying to involve the player subconsciously thanks to themes relying upon these natural instincts and emotions.

Clearly, this is the trickiest part in designing a successful game, and we will try to learn something more about it by analyzing the case studies that will follow by means of our framework. If the designer is successful in this endeavor, the game will most likely feel immersive and going through its challenges will provide players with a rewarding experience. In other words, this will deliver what most people feel is a fun experience.

Then, once the playing session is over, we will get into Phase 3 where the player subconsciously feels satisfied for the time spent playing. This will, in turn, trigger some different emotions like pride (if successful) or delusion (if things didn't go too well this time). In any case, the instinct for improving ourselves, our results, and doing better than our friends (competition!), or just the wish to get more in depth into the game and experience some new events or facets of the story will kick in by giving the right motivation to come back to the game at a later time, bringing the player back to Phase 2.

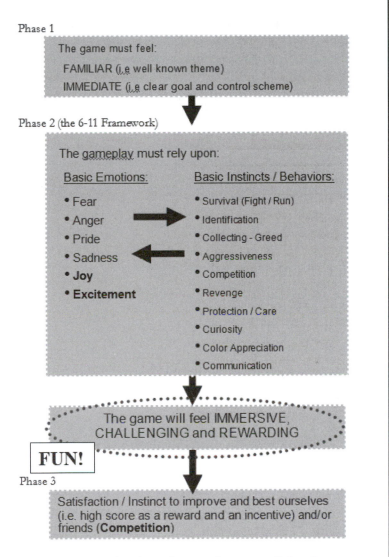

Figure 3. Emotional analysis of a gameplay session. Before the game (Phase 1), capture the attention; during the game (Phase 2), bring in emotions for immersion and, ultimately, fun. After the game (Phase 3), rely on competition and rewards to bring players back.

Note that this natural looping mechanism can sometimes become very intense and result in so-called "gaming addiction" that can have detrimental, even dangerous, consequences. Gaming addiction is being addressed very seriously these days, from both medical and gaming perspectives. In fact, modern games like MMOs now tend to feature shorter quests to encourage players to take breaks and rest.

Figure 3 summarizes the different phases of a successful gameplay session as described so far.

Making Fun Games the Emotional Way

In the previous section we have seen that a game needs to be immersive and challenging to be fun. To achieve this, we need to structure it so that we can successfully induce an exciting situation for the player by manipulating the game flow through different emotions, which, in turn, are reached by exploiting our common instincts. How do we do this?

First and foremost, remember we have to make players interested in our game and show them it's not going to be that hard to get into it. Once we choose a subject players can easily relate to (familiarity and identification) and have designed the control system to be immediate and easy to grasp, the real challenge to take the player on a fun journey begins. Here is where we have to carefully consider the different emotions and instincts we want to arouse during gameplay and design the corresponding game dynamics accordingly.

For example, a possible way to reach fun in a hypothetical game would be to immerse the player in a beautiful and colorful environment. This will resonate with our color-appreciation instinct that, besides giving the player an initial sense of satisfaction/joy, will also help trigger the curiosity instinct, thanks also to the identification we already set up, driving the player to explore the surroundings. Once this happens, a fearful emotional state can be induced by a sudden encounter with some hostile creature, triggering the survival instincts with consequent excitement for the battle and confrontation.

This sort of emotional sequence, or path, that we will now call "On the Way To Fun" can be derived by analyzing the flow of the game in terms of the 6-11 Framework, and it can ultimately be used to describe and predict players' emotional engagement.

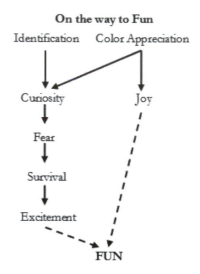

On the way to Fun

Identification   Color Appreciation

Curiosity   Joy

Fear

Survival

Excitement

FUN

Figure 4. On the Way To Fun diagram. An emotional scheme for describing players' subconscious emotional engagement and progression by analyzing the effects of game dynamics through the 6-11 Framework. (The dashed lines leading to fun from the final emotions will not be shown in future diagrams.)

A possible path for the previous example is shown in Figure 4. In the end, a game that successfully delivers an emotional experience like this is likely to be considered immersive, enjoyable, and, ultimately, fun.

It is also important to note that apart from ending with excitement and/or joy, our "ways to fun" should usually start by triggering an instinct first and not by raising an emotion right away. The reason is that by relying on an instinct first, we push the player to perform some action by his own will. This is part of the identification process and, in turn, it will provoke the arousal of some related emotion. In this way the player will have the

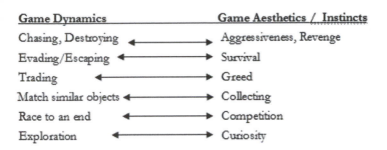

Game Dynamics		Game Aesthetics / Instincts
Chasing, Destroying	⟷	Aggressiveness, Revenge
Evading/Escaping	⟷	Survival
Trading	⟷	Greed
Match similar objects	⟷	Collecting
Race to an end	⟷	Competition
Exploration	⟷	Curiosity

Figure 5. Matching a few common game dynamics with their related aesthetics/instincts.

feeling of being in charge and, whatever happens, he will believe it was as a direct consequence of his own actions.

If, on the other hand, we were to start off by triggering an emotion (e.g., the game starts and the player is suddenly attacked by a hidden monster for no reason whatsoever), we would obviously induce a reaction from him but he would feel more passive and not really involved in what's going on. To avoid this pitfall, let's constantly remind ourselves that videogames are an interactive media and, as such, we must empower the players within the constraints of the virtual worlds we define (or at least give them such an illusion!).

Regarding game dynamics, we can easily see that in the previous example we had an exploration and then, according to the player's reactions, an escaping or fighting dynamic after being attacked by the monster. Obviously, there can be countless ways to craft a dynamic to match and relate to an emotional aspect of the game, as boundaries are set only by the designer's own imagination.

A sample of possible correspondences between some well-known game dynamics and instincts is exemplified in Figure 5 while other examples will be shown within each case study.

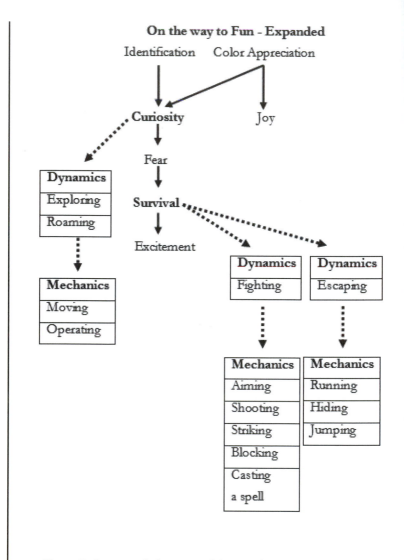

Figure 6. An expanded version of the On the Way To Fun diagram proposed in Figure 4, now including game dynamics and mechanics which are triggered by the corresponding aesthetics (in bold).

Note that the relationship between instincts and dynamics should be considered as bi-directional; while the emergence of a particular dynamic can be used to excite an instinct, we can also observe that it is often an emotion-triggered instinct that pushes the player towards a specific dynamic, like survival—pushing the player to fight for his life in the previous example. By adopting a MDA-like approach, we can see how this close relationship between instincts and game dynamics allows us to easily relate these two aspects within the 6-11 Framework. We can then expand the On the Way To Fun diagram accordingly by including the latter and the underlying mechanics. Figure 6 provides a quick graphical analysis representing the whole game emotional structure and playing experience.

Through the examples that will follow, we will see how this whole process was achieved, both by big companies in the past and by some of the most talented indie game developers of today. Understanding how the games we analyze implemented different dynamics to rely on particular instinctive and emotional aspects of our psyche—as depicted by the corresponding On the Way To Fun diagrams—can surely inspire and teach us a lot about how to create engaging entertainment experiences.

PART II

Case Studies: Retro Games

Examples of early home computers and retro gaming systems. From top left clockwise: Sinclair ZX81 (1981), Mattel Intellivision (1979), Atari VCS/2600 (1977), and the Commodore VIC-20 (1981).

Why Retro Games?

Now we will try to figure out how to apply the ideas explained so far in actual games. We will do so by using the 6-11 Framework to analyze how these ideas were implemented in real commercial products and how their game dynamics were successfully built around basic emotions and instincts. In particular, we will review and analyze a set of meaningful games for different systems, including early home computers, video game consoles, and arcade machines. This means we will be looking at the very beginning of what is nowadays known as the "retro game" scene. But why did we choose games that are so old in the first place? There are several reasons for this apparently odd choice.

First, these games are much simpler than modern ones, so the ideas they are built upon are much easier to identify, analyze individually, and, ultimately, understand. In fact, since the technical constraints of the time didn't allow for realistic graphics and sound effects, early games had to rely exclusively on their gameplay qualities to capture players' attention. In other words, gameplay was king and this meant that game dynamics were much more exposed and more easily appreciated. Interestingly, this simplicity is very relevant today because it makes old games like these very close to today's casual and indie productions, at least in spirit, where simple yet addictive gameplay can determine the success of a game while fancy effects are not that important. Finally, there is also a small nostalgia factor—I'm sure many of these older games will likely prompt some fond memories in readers in their mid-thirties. Reading about them, then, will hopefully not only be instructive by providing some interesting ideas and inspiration to modern indie developers, but also fun and entertaining.

Computer Space and *Space Invaders* original arcade machines.

Computer Space
1971, Nutting Associates

Space Invaders
1978, Taito

Aesthetics	Dynamics	Mechanics	Other
aggressiveness	fighting	moving	familiarity
immediateness		shooting	immediateness
protection		hiding	

For our first example, let's start with a comparison of two early arcade games. *Computer Space*, released by Nutting Associates, was the first commercial arcade game designed by Nolan Bushnell before he founded Atari with Ted Dabney a few months later. *Space Invaders*, on the other hand, was released by Taito in 1978.

The former wasn't very successful while the second was a huge hit worldwide. Why? Besides timing reasons (we shouldn't forget that Computer Space was the first coin-operated game ever and therefore had to build its audience from scratch, which is never an easy task), let's see what else could have determined their different fortunes by analyzing how they implemented the features and characteristics we've discussed.

Both games are set in space, featuring battles with aliens. Was this sort of setting familiar at the time the games were released? Absolutely. In fact, at least among teenagers and young adults, space adventures were quite popular thanks to the sci-fi literature and many comic books that were hugely successful from the 1960s onward.

But are both games immediate? The goal is clear enough in both (shoot the aliens and avoid being hit) but what about the controls? Here is where the two games depart from each other quite significantly. While *Space Invaders* features a simple joystick (the player only needs to move left and right) and one fire button, *Computer Space* has a fairly complex control scheme with four independent buttons to rotate the ship, thrust, and shoot. Obviously, the former requires no effort to be understood even by an absolute beginner or a casual passerby and this feature contributed significantly to making the game more appealing

Computer Space vs. Space Invaders

to a broad range of people. On the other hand, the control scheme for *Computer Space* most likely felt quite intimidating to the average gamer in the early to mid-1970s, preventing it from being a bigger hit.

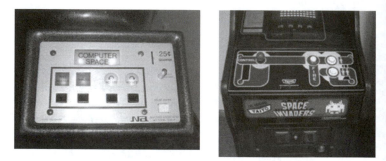

Controls for *Computer Space* (left) and *Space Invaders*(right). Which set is more immediate?

Moving on to Phase 2, or the analysis of the actual gameplay by applying the 6-11 Framework, we see how both games rely on aggressiveness (destroying aliens) but it is more effective in *Space Invaders* where we have the impression of defending our planet. This gives us the feeling of protecting the whole human race from an invasion of some hostile creatures which not only provides a clear objective to the game (relying on the protection instinct) but it also adds to the overall immediateness thanks to the easy link between the goal and how to achieve it through the proposed control scheme. This aspect is completely absent in *Computer Space* where the battle takes place in the void of some galaxy far, far away. Overall, we can say that *Computer Space* failed to appeal to more players due to the complex nature of its controls coupled with the lack of motivation to justify players' aggressiveness.

To conclude, let's look at a simple On the Way To Fun diagram for *Space Invaders*.

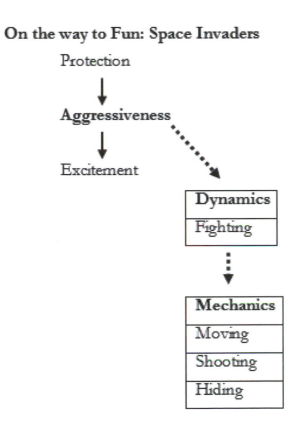

On the way to Fun: Space Invaders

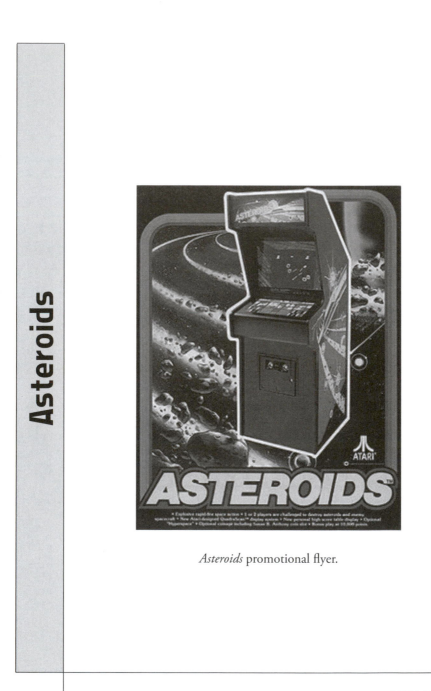

Asteroids promotional flyer.

Aesthetics	Dynamics	Mechanics
competition	destroying	breaking
pride	escaping	shooting
survival	maneuvering	rotating
		thrusting
		hyperspace jumping

One of the biggest hits in the arcades in the late seventies and early eighties was *Asteroids*, a game developed by Atari.

This game, where we had to go through a never-ending belt of asteroids, had an even more complex control scheme than *Computer Space*. In fact, yet another button ("hyperspace", to make the player's ship jump to a random place on the screen) was added to *Asteroids* to bring the total to five, without any input from a joystick. Obviously, although the game objective was immediate (survive the asteroids by shooting at them and breaking them into smaller pieces until they are completely destroyed) that was not true of the controls, which were likely the main culprit for the failure of *Computer Space*. So why was *Asteroids* successful? There are two main reasons that made people willing to play again and again while putting in more effort to overcome the unintuitive controls.

First, *Asteroids* came out in 1979—eight years after *Computer Space's* debut. At that time, though still in their infancy, video games were not an absolute novelty anymore and we can say that a first group of "hardcore" gamers were born. They were ready to spend more time to get accustomed to different control schemes.

Second, and even more important, *Asteroids* was absolutely fantastic in triggering the competitive instinct of players. Before *Asteroids*, games were only able to record the top high score but nothing else. *Asteroids* introduced a small leader-board where players could see the top scores and the names or three-letter nicknames (nicks) of the people who achieved them. So

Asteroids

Asteroids was the first game in which players could feel pride and be acknowledged for their results. This characteristic, obviously, kept reinforcing the competitive aspects of the game, with players putting a lot of effort toward improving their personal best and beating their friends and rivals at the arcade, thus gaining the right to write their own nick on top of others'. It's no surprise that the first videogame tournaments and marathon exhibitions to achieve world high-score records were organized using this game and that leader-boards to showcase players results have been featured ever since.

As we see from the diagram, already in the late seventies games were relying on different instincts in parallel (in this case survival and competition) thanks to different features. Note also that these instincts could be related to something external to the actual playing session (like a leader-board) but they could still play a big role in keeping players excited and interested even after the game was over.

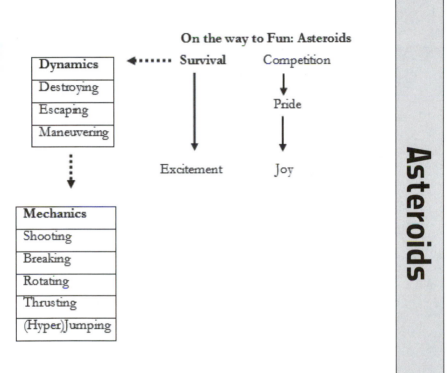

On the way to Fun: Asteroids

Asteroids

Battlezone

Original promotional flyer from Atari.

Aesthetics	Dynamics	Mechanics
aggressiveness	fighting	shooting
identification	maneuvering	aiming
fear		moving
		stopping
		turning

Battlezone was a groundbreaking game as it was one of earliest arcades to showcase a real three-dimensional vector-based environment. The game itself was fairly simple; the player maneuvered a tank and had to face one enemy at a time in a sort of duel. Its innovative first-person view greatly increased its evocative qualities and with them, its appeal and the ability to make players really identify with the tank's commander.

The scene, though extremely simple and stylized, was very impressive, featuring mountains on the horizon, an erupting volcano, a crescent moon, and various geometric solids like pyramids and blocks. The settings, in fact, were so good and believable that people really felt completely immersed in the virtual world. Magazines even started getting mail from young readers asking if they "could reach the mountains or the volcano" in the game to see if "there were enemy bases over there," not realizing that they were just a backdrop!

The in-game action could become quite intense and the sight of a hostile tank turning toward us and shooting at us was emotionally very effective and…scary, exciting the survival instinct and pushing the player to shoot at the enemy while maneuvering to avoid the incoming projectiles. Besides these qualities, a high-score table was included, like in *Asteroids*, allowing players to compete with friends and strangers to see who was the best shooter in the arcade.

From the diagram we can see how *Battlezone* successfully used all of these features to enhance players' emotional experience starting from a very similar model to the one used in

Battlezone

Asteroids but by adding a stronger identification element thanks to the first-person perspective. Ultimately, *Battlezone's* immersive qualities made it a very popular and successful game for several years and justified the porting to many home computers and systems, such as the Apple II, Commodore 64, ZX Spectrum, and others including those, like the Atari 2600, that couldn't support vector graphics due to technical limitations and had to use a simpler colored raster approach.

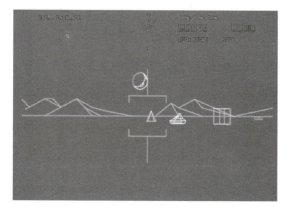

The moon, the mountains, and a menacing tank pointing at us… that's *Battlezone*!

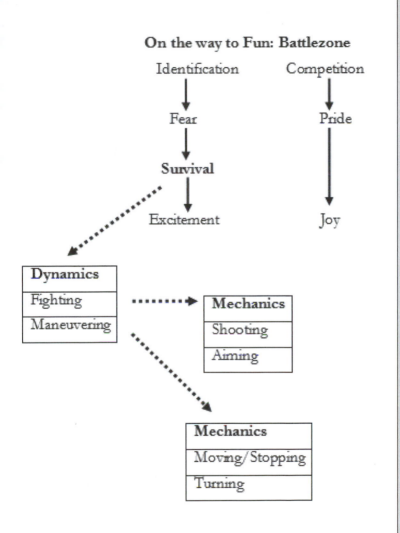

On the way to Fun: Battlezone

Identification → Fear → **Survival** → Excitement

Competition → Pride → Joy

Dynamics
| Fighting |
| Maneuvering |

Mechanics
| Shooting |
| Aiming |

Mechanics
| Moving/Stopping |
| Turning |

Battlezone

Pac-Man

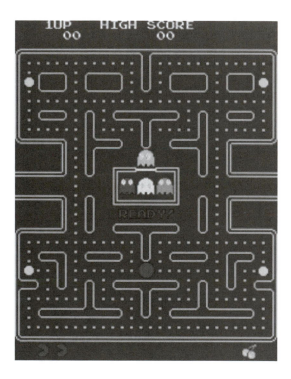

Screenshot from the original *Pac-Man* arcade game.
Ready, set, go! The game begins!

1980, Namco

Aesthetics	Dynamics	Mechanics
anger	escaping	moving
collecting	chasing	eating/taking
revenge	attacking	
survival	reaching	

Who doesn't know *Pac-Man*—the game developed by Namco (first released in Japan on May 22, 1980) where the player had to eat all dots in a maze while being chased by four cute ghosts? *Pac-Man* wasn't only one of the most successful games ever, spawning sequels, clones, and ports to any imaginable system, but it was also the very first game to turn into a "brand"; t-shirts, mugs, plush toys, and many other objects were produced featuring its yellow dot-eating "thing" and its colorful rivals, many of which can still be found today, thirty years after its original release.

At first sight, the game looks fairly simple so what could be the reasons for its incredible success? First, its simple but colorful graphics were very easy to understand and appreciate. They clearly resonated with our color appreciation instinct, making people interested in the game and happy to start playing it. The main character, while extremely nondescript, was also funny and cute, which made it easy for all players to identify with it and somewhat scared by the ghosts chasing after it.

As we know, the aim of the game was to "eat" all the tiny dots on the screen, which relates to our collection instinct. Additionally, different fruit bonus items could appear for a short period of time, pushing players to collect them whenever possible. This greedy behavior could also generate excitement in the players. For example, a player may approach a bonus that could disappear at any time—possibly just a fraction of a second before the player reached it—leaving him in a dangerous situation with a nearby ghost.

Furthermore, the so-called "power-pellets" (the bigger dots at the corner of the screen) allowed Pac-Man to chase the ghosts

Pac-Man

for a short while and eat them instead of being eaten by them as usual. This feature allowed for a very interesting twist. For most of the game, the player was under pressure and it was his survival instinct of escaping from the ghosts which drove him across the maze. Likely, he would start feeling angry at those relentless ghosts always chasing after him but then, suddenly, here comes the chance of releasing such anger and get the proper revenge by becoming the chaser and going after the monsters instead!

From the On the Way to Fun diagram we can appreciate how even an apparently simple game like *Pac-Man* can actually hide a relatively complex network of aesthetics. Arguably, an important part of its everlasting appeal was due to successfully relying on several emotions and instincts that enhanced and effectively interacted with each other to provide a new, exciting, and joyful experience. Amazingly, we can also notice how all of this happened with only two game mechanics—moving around the maze and eating (taking) the dots and, when possible, the ghosts. Really a beautiful example of obtaining the maximum result with a minimum set of tools! Last, we shouldn't forget about *Pac-Man's* two player competitive mode, which gave players many opportunities for exciting head-to-head competition.

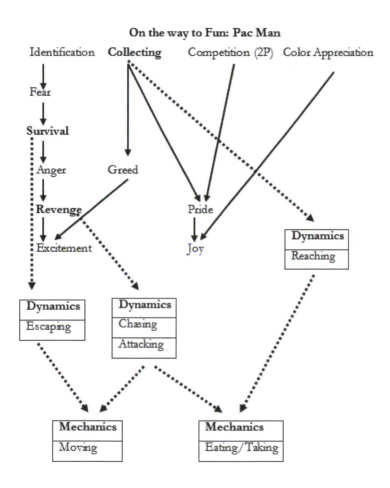

On the way to Fun: Pac Man

Pac-Man

Aesthetics	Dynamics	Mechanics	Other
anger	attacking	shooting	familiarity
identification	conversing	moving	
protection	searching	rotating	
communication	saving	taking	
revenge		talking	

Although today this game is mostly forgotten, *Rescue at Rigel*, developed by Epyx for several home computers (Apple II, TRS-80, VIC-20, Atari 8-bit, and DOS), is still worth remembering since it showcased some interesting elements.

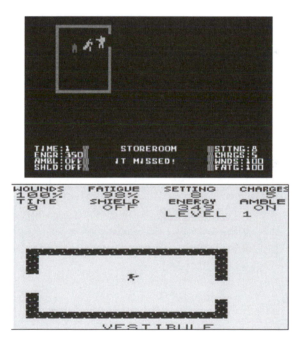

Atari 8 bit screenshot (top) and the VIC-20 version (bottom).

Rescue at Rigel

Rescue at Rigel was the first RPG set in space. The player, an agent named Sudden Smith, had to rescue ten humans held captive by aliens in a space base having 60 rooms spread across six floors and with only 60 minutes to accomplish the mission. Despite the very poor graphics, the game made an effort to let the player identify with the main character and to make him feel personally involved in the story and action.

In fact, the whole plot idea was clearly and strongly related to events that were of extreme and serious importance for Americans in 1980; in particular, the reference was to the so-called "Iran Hostage Crisis,"* a very serious diplomatic incident that created strong tension between the United States and Iran. This was evident from the alien-abductors' names—the "Tollah" and their chief, the "High Tollah," an apparent link to the Iranian leader of the time, the Ayatollah Ruhollah Khomeini.

These references were designed to make the game more familiar and immerse players in an otherwise odd story, making them angry and revengeful, while relying on the protection instinct for the guys who were kidnapped. Anger was also enhanced by a cunning use of the communication instinct—the game also gives the theoretical chance to try to end the conflict peacefully by talking to the aliens. This never really happens though, making the player even more frustrated and angry. Note also that the time limit and resulting pressure was an important element for adding overall excitement and a sense of urgency to the experience—a characteristic we will find in many other games, including today's productions.

*November 4, 1979–January 20, 1981. See http://en.wikipedia.org/wiki/Iran_hostage_crisis for a quick review of what happened.

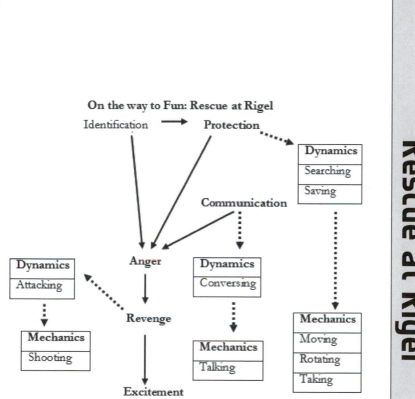

On the way to Fun: Rescue at Rigel

Haunted House

1981, Atari

Aesthetics	Dynamics	Mechanics
curiosity	escaping	moving
fear	exploring	operating (using light)
survival	searching	taking
collecting	choosing	dropping

Haunted House was a very interesting game for the Atari 2600; it is regarded as the first example of the "survival horror" genre. In *Haunted House*, the player, represented by a pair of wide-open eyes, had to navigate a creepy old manor spreading across different floors and in absolute darkness to find three pieces of an ancient urn. The house is infested by bats, tarantulas, and ghosts that can be kept at a distance by using a magical scepter to be found somewhere in one of the rooms. Several doors are locked but somewhere in the house, a master key can be found. To help the player in his quest, he can use an unlimited number of matches to light up a small zone around him and see if there is any object worth taking.

The game obviously relied on the familiarity of the "haunted house" horror movies that were very popular in the seventies and early eighties, and the game based its gameplay on the curiosity of exploring the manor together with the collecting instinct of retrieving all the pieces of the precious urn. In doing so, it also tried to bring the player into an uncomfortable situation thanks to the total darkness of the environment and, eventually, to scare him with the sudden appearances of some monsters.

In this example we see how the game tried to achieve fun by having two different emotional paths, both originating from the curiosity instinct and leading to excitement and to joy, respectively. The exploration path, with its exciting dangers, worked side by side with the collection of the urn pieces, which would make the player proud and happy for his progress and, ultimately, successful reconstruction of the urn.

Haunted House

Despite the clever use of the available resources, the graphics were considered too basic to really scare the player. And the idea of having the player represented by a pair of big eyes tended to be a bit too cute and funny to match the creepy atmosphere for which the game seemed to aim. These may be some of the reasons why *Haunted House* didn't actually get the attention and success it deserved, but the biggest problem was clearly the complete lack of a scoring system. This was a serious flaw that halted all competiveness between players and, most likely, made them decide to challenge each other in other games.

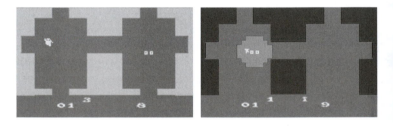

Screenshots from the game. Darkness with a glowing ghost (left) and after having lit a match to find a piece of the urn (right).

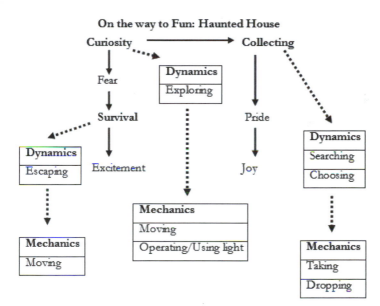

On the way to Fun: Haunted House

Curiosity ⟶ Collecting

Fear

Dynamics
Exploring

Survival

Pride

Dynamics
Escaping

Excitement

Joy

Dynamics
Searching
Choosing

Mechanics
Moving

Mechanics
Moving
Operating/Using light

Mechanics
Taking
Dropping

Haunted House

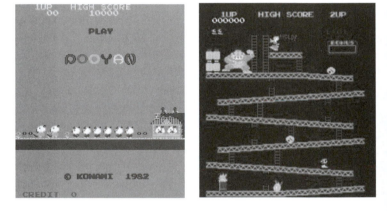

Pooyan (left) and Donkey Kong (right) represent examples of how the same instinct (protection, in this case) can be related to completely different genres (shooter vs. platformer) and game mechanics (shooting vs. running and jumping).

Aesthetics	Dynamics	Mechanics	Other
protection	defending	moving	familiarity
joy (through rewards)		shooting	

The arcade game *Pooyan* by Konami, released in 1982, is a shooter that is based on the protection instinct, one of the most overly used instincts in games and that we will find quite often among productions across all consoles and systems in any given hardware generation. In this game, our goal is not as ambitious as protecting the whole world or even other fellow human beings. Instead, we have to defend little cute pigs from hordes of hungry wolves who want to kidnap (and likely eat) them. Note how this simple setting makes the game instantly familiar—who didn't hear stories and fairy tales about small pigs and bad wolves throughout his or her childhood?

This game, like others that came out around the same time such as *Donkey Kong* (Nintendo, 1981),* also featured some simple cut scenes in between levels to reward players for their successes. *Pooyan* is also notable for having a bonus stage after every two levels, giving a chance to safely increase the player's own high score.

All of these new features not only gave players a reason to keep playing to see the next cut scene, but they also made players happier as it gave a sort of "visual prize" for their successful efforts, plus a few seconds to relax before the next attack wave. In addition to the now-usual high-score table, a competitive two-player mode, where friends alternate playing to challenge each other, was available, increasing the challenge and replayability of the game.

Pooyan

*Interestingly, even though it is a platformer and not a shooter, *Donkey Kong* still relies on exactly the same protection instinct as does *Pooyan*. In *Donkey Kong*'s case, though, we have to protect/rescue a damsel in distress and not little pigs!

Although not many people fondly remember *Pooyan* nowadays, it had relatively good success, especially in Japan. It was ported to several consoles and home computers (e.g., Atari 2600, NES, C64, MSX, Apple II) and spawned a few (forgettable) clones like Mastertronic's *Pigs in Space* for the Commodore 64 (1984), which I personally had the misfortune of buying and playing many years ago. *Pooyan* even gave rise to a board game.

The original arcade *Pooyan* in action (left) and the C64 version of *Pigs in Space* (right), one of the clones that *Pooyan* spawned.

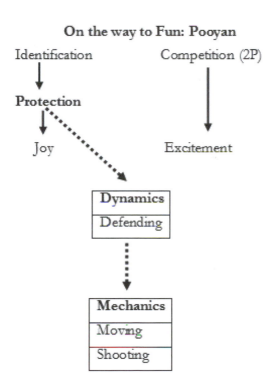

On the way to Fun: Pooyan

Identification   Competition (2P)

Protection

Joy   Excitement

| **Dynamics** |
| Defending |

| **Mechanics** |
| Moving |
| Shooting |

Pooyan

Robotron 2084

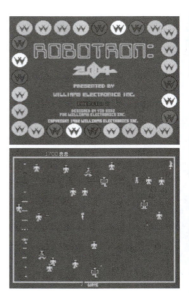

Aesthetics	Dynamics	Mechanics
anger	attacking	moving
color appreciation	fighting	aiming
identification	escaping	shooting
joy	reaching	taking
protection	saving	
revenge		
survival		

As in one of his previous games for Williams Electronics (*Defender*, 1980), game designer and developer Eugene Jarvis decided to add a protection element in *Robotron 2084* to make the overall experience more meaningful to players. This was a wise choice as this theme, together with the hectic action of the game plus its original and challenging (but still intuitive) controls, made *Robotron 2084* one of most well-known arcade games ever and still inspires developers to this day.

We've mentioned the controls system in some of our games. In several of his designs, Jarvis tried to go beyond the common and overly simplistic "joystick plus button" scheme. Already in *Defender*, an excellent space shooter where the player had to fight alien ships while also saving helpless humanoids on the ground from being captured, he designed an original scheme featuring a joystick plus five buttons. Unfortunately, this scheme was perceived as too difficult by many but despite this (or maybe thanks to this), *Defender* succeeded in developing a user-dedicated fan base among hardcore gamers who kept playing it throughout the eighties, guaranteeing its lasting success.

With *Robotron*, on the other hand, Jarvis tried something a little more intuitive. The game used two eight-sided directional joysticks with no buttons at all. While the left joystick controlled the character's movement, the right one controlled the direction of the character's weapon firing. This proved to be a challenging,

Robotron 2084

but fun, exercise in two hands and eye coordination that most people felt was different but not too hard to understand and try.

There were other underlying elements that become apparent when playing *Robotron* and that were fundamental in determining its success. For example, the game tried very hard to make players identify with the super-human character they had to play by presenting him in a dedicated screenshot while explaining the game's plot. At the same time, besides their own safety and survival, the game tried to make players care about the "last human family" whose members (mommy, daddy, Mickey, and a couple of other unnamed relatives) walk around panicking while hordes of robotrons chase after them. Once this caring relationship was properly set up, players would likely feel happy when saving them and angry when family members are killed, thus expanding the range of emotions that could be conveyed by the game itself.

All of this was achieved through the clever use of simple, but colorful and flashy graphics. The graphics were intended to attract players in dark arcades from a distance by relying on our color appreciation and curiosity instincts and then drive them smoothly into the excitement of the action.

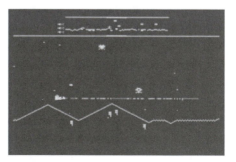

A screenshot from the arcade game *Defender*.

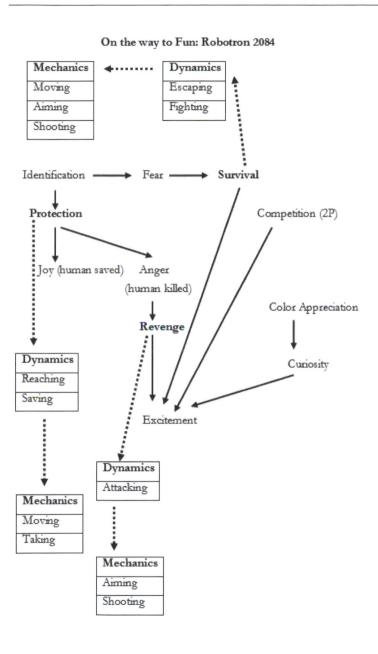

On the way to Fun: Robotron 2084

Pitfall!

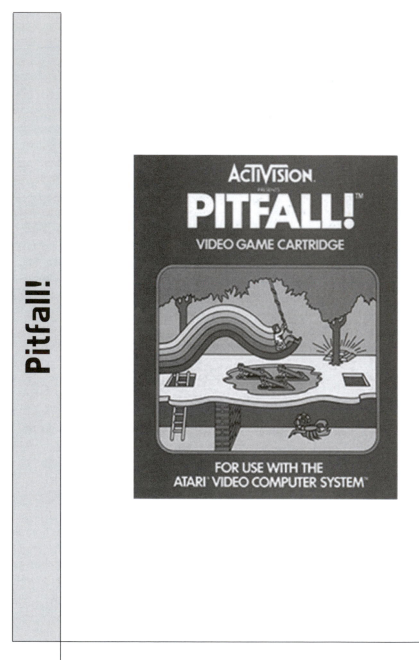

Aesthetics	Dynamics	Mechanics	Other
collecting	exploring	running	familiarity
color	searching	jumping	
appreciation		taking	
curiosity		choosing a path	
identification			

Pifall!, by Activision's co-founder David Crane, was one of the greatest successes on home consoles at the time, first published on the Atari 2600 and then ported to many other systems.

The idea of playing as Pitfall Harry, a young explorer lost in a remote jungle filled with wild beasts and dangers to collect 32 treasures in only 20 minutes, was immediately familiar thanks to references to characters like Tarzan (when swinging over a vine we can hear something clearly inspired by Tarzan's characteristic cry), cartoons like *Heckle and Jekyll*, and movies such as the then recently released Indiana Jones adventure, *Raiders of the Lost Ark* (1981). Thanks to all of these references, it was very straightforward for players to identify with the in-game character and his quest.

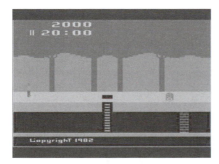

The game also showcased very rich and colorful graphics, with smooth animations that were far better than anything seen up to that time on the Atari machine. This obviously stimulated a player's curiosity to see the next screen (there were 254

in total) and its dangers, like quicksand, lakes, pits, rolling logs, bats, scorpions, and crocodiles, while also looking for the next treasure to collect (gold, diamonds, etc.).

Here the collecting instinct was obviously one of the main aesthetics defining the player's emotional experience, and it was expressed through searching the environment (dynamic) to pick up the different objects (mechanic). At the same time, excitement due to the time pressure constantly mounted, providing a truly unique experience that really immersed the players deeply into the adventure.

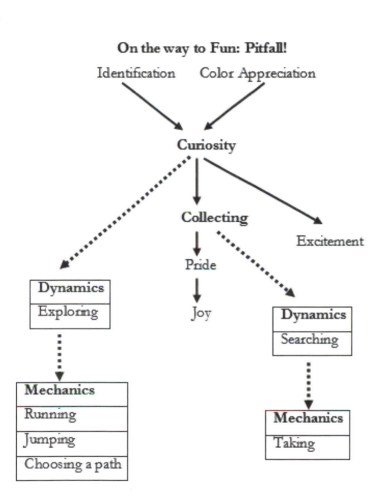

On the way to Fun: Pitfall!

Identification   Color Appreciation

Curiosity

Collecting

Excitement

Pride

Dynamics
Exploring

Joy

Dynamics
Searching

Mechanics
Running
Jumping
Choosing a path

Mechanics
Taking

Pitfall!

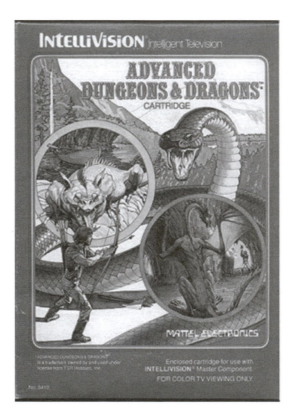

Aesthetics	Dynamics	Mechanics	Other
collecting	exploring	moving	familiarity
curiosity	escaping	running	
fear	fighting	choosing a path	
greed	searching	shooting	
identification		aiming	
survival		taking	

After a couple of experiments on mainframes and supercomputers, in 1982 the famous *Advanced Dungeons and Dragons* (*AD&D*) series of table role-playing games (started in 1974 by TSR Inc.), where players were immersed in a fantasy world filled with dangerous mazes and lands looking for fame and fortune, finally got an adaptation for a widespread home video-gaming system, the Intellivision. In *Cloudy Mountain*, we were required to recover the lost "Crown of Kings" which was broken into two pieces with each piece guarded by a scary and fierce dragon. Needless to say, to accomplish our mission we had to explore a series of randomly generated dungeons and face dangers no one before had ever survived. The branded name and setting made the game instantly familiar to players with a passion for the *AD&D* games and, while the controls would feel awkward to non-Intellivision players, they were quite standard for those who owned the Mattel console.

Intellivision's games, instead of a simple control scheme based on an eight-directional joystick plus button, had a disk capable of identifying 16 directions, four shoulder buttons and a small keyboard featuring 12 buttons. The functions for the buttons changed from game to game and were identified by thin overlays to be put on the keys, like the one in the next figure. In this particular game, arrows were shot in the direction pointed by the button (e.g., pressing 2 would shoot upward), while the shoulder buttons were used to run in the direction pointed by the disk. We can probably say that this relatively complex but

Advanced Dungeons & Dragons: Cloudy Mountain

flexible control system made the Intellivision the first "hard-core" gaming system.

Cloudy Mountain was notable for its very smart use of visual and audio cues to elicit a strong curiosity instinct and, at times, a very strong sense of fear in the player. The mission started on a big map where the player's party (three flashing dots, each

The world map where the adventure begins.
Not an easy journey to Cloudy Mountain!

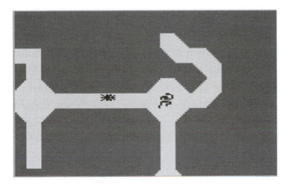

Running away from a spider. Note the "shroud of darkness" above the player—what's hiding over there, safety, or an even worse danger?

representing a party member—three lives) could move and explore the land and choose a suitable path towards cloudy mountain. To reach it, though, they had to get through several smaller mountains, each featuring a dungeon.

Once in a dungeon, the fun began. Visually, only the small portion of the maze centered on the player was displayed, in addition to already-explored areas. This was the first implementation ever of the so-called "shroud of darkness" (which is today also called "fog of war"), an effect that became a fundamental element in many games that followed, including modern RPGs and real-time strategy (RTS) games.

The shroud of darkness contributed significantly in increasing players' curiosity to keep exploring the maze and with it, also raised the fear that some terrible creature could be hiding in the darkness just around the corner waiting. . . .

This creepy atmosphere was further enhanced by effective in-game sounds that, even though simple and rudimentary by today's standards, successfully added a sense of uneasiness by letting the player hear nearby creatures even if unseen. If a snake were nearby, we'd hear a hissing sound, if there were bats, we'd

Advanced Dungeons & Dragons: Cloudy Mountain

hear a flapping sound (which would dangerously cover all other sounds), and so on. Then, when an enemy suddenly appeared and attacked the player, fear kicked in, triggering his survival instinct as he had to quickly decide whether to escape or fight back by shooting arrows that could, eventually, bounce back off the wall and even hit the player himself! All of these elements, together with the greed instinct motivating us to search for different treasures and items, made this game a very exciting and entertaining experience.

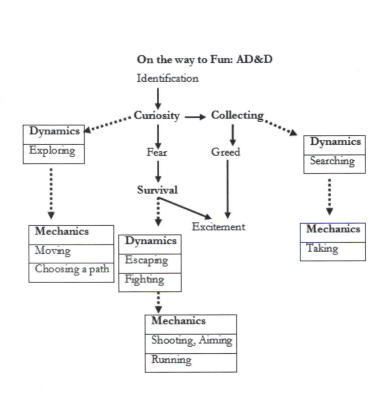

On the way to Fun: AD&D

Advanced Dungeons & Dragons: Cloudy Mountain

3D Monster Maze

J. K. GREYE SOFTWARE

3D
MONSTER MAZE

GAMESTAPE 4

for 16K ZX81

Aesthetics	Dynamics	Mechanics	Other
curiosity	exploring	moving	familiarity
fear	escaping	running	
identification		turning	
survival		choosing a path	

Programmed in 1981 by Malcolm Evans on a Sinclair ZX 81, *3D Monster Maze* was probably the most amazing and exciting game for a home computer in the early eighties. In fact, it managed not only to simulate a three-dimensional, first-person view, but it did so on one of the cheapest and most limited home computers available at the time (though expanded to 16 KB of RAM)! The first-person perspective greatly enhanced players' identification feelings, allowing for an unprecedented immersive experience among home-based entertainment.

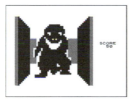

3D Monster Maze was one of the very first games on a home computer to showcase a first-person perspective.

Evans didn't stop there. He wanted his game to also feel familiar from the very beginning. Actually, the game was about escaping from a maze while being chased by a...T-Rex! I doubt this experience could sound familiar to the average guy in the early eighties, as the dinosaur craze, started by movies like *Jurassic Park*, had yet to come. Nonetheless, legends based on mazes and monsters like the minotaur could provide some sort of background support and, in addition, Evans also had a very clever idea to make the game feel even more familiar, fun, and attractive—he introduced it as an attraction in a carnival setting!

This narrative trick turned the original unusual concept into a fun, mysterious, and attractive one that players suddenly felt familiar with and curious about. Once the player gets into the randomly generated maze, he realizes the T-Rex isn't just a silicon reproduction, as claimed by the cunning carnival guy, but it is actually the real thing and…it is hungry!

Introducing the game as a carnival attraction—even a T-Rex wouldn't be so strange anymore and it would make players curious and willing to get into the maze to explore it.

The immersion level, reached thanks to the first-person perspective, enhanced the fear emotion about being chased and this, together with the subsequent survival (flight/run) instinct, were the main driving forces while playing the game. Tension and excitement levels were increased even further by the clever use of text messages telling the player something about the T-Rex status. In particular, players were notified of the following:

- REX LIES IN WAIT
- HE IS HUNTING FOR YOU
- FOOTSTEPS APPROACHING
- REX HAS SEEN YOU
- RUN! HE IS BESIDE YOU
- RUN! HE IS BEHIND YOU

These simple messages had another big emotional impact and added the final seal in conveying a sense of urgency and danger never before seen on a home computer. Computer magazines of the time reported the experiences of several players who accidentally reset the machine or even broke the keyboard of the ZX81 due to pressing too hard in the excitement of the escape!

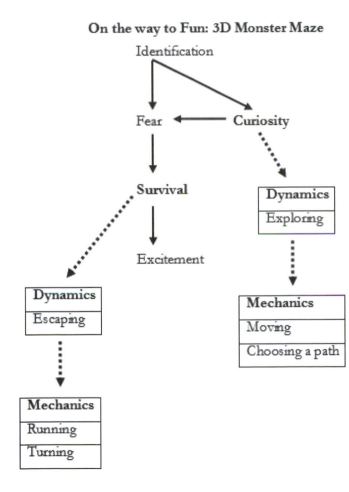

On the way to Fun: 3D Monster Maze

3D Monster Maze

E.T. the Extra-Terrestrial

1982, Atari

Aesthetics	Dynamics	Mechanics	Other
collecting	escaping	moving	familiarity
identification	searching	running	
survival	running	jumping	
protection	herding	taking	

So far, with the exception of *Computer Space* and, to some extent, *Haunted House*, we have analyzed only games that were fully successful in reaching their goals and in providing exciting and fun experiences to players. So it's high time now to look at a game that is still considered to be the biggest fiasco in the history of gaming—*E.T. the Extra-Terrestrial* (E.T.) for the Atari 2600

E.T. case (opposite page) and splash screen (above), are considered by many to be the best parts of the game.

The game had to be developed in just a few weeks by Howard Scott Warshaw to be ready for the holiday season and exploit the popularity of the E.T. movie, which was the craze of the moment. Movie tie-ins with games were getting more and more common at the time and this certainly made the game instantly familiar and appealing.

The gameplay was based around the collection instinct as the player, by taking the role of E.T., had to find three pieces of his phone to call the aliens who would come back to pick him up. Things were made difficult by two characters chasing E.T.,

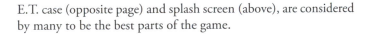

E.T. the Extra-Terrestrial

Many wells to choose from, but all equally boring (while Elliot tries to help by leaving some Reese's Pieces candy to replenish E.T.'s energies).

an agent and a scientist, to take E.T. back to their own bases for questioning and analysis purposes. This event would make E.T. lose precious time and energy but luckily, Elliot (the boy in the movie) could also be called at times to help and replenish the player's energy level.

In playing the game, two problems became quickly apparent. The controls and user interface were extremely confusing. There were many indicators and things to do but it was very difficult to figure how things worked. In an Italian magazine published in early 1983,* the reviewers got a preview copy of the game but without the instructions booklet, with the result that they couldn't figure out some of the functions and successfully end the game, despite all their efforts.

Second, the three phone pieces the player had to find were randomly scattered in some wells. These wells, which were not in the movie, were a real chore to jump out of and the player had really to struggle and try many times before he could jump out successfully without falling back in again and again.

The game's biggest problem existed at the very core of its design—in the identification area. In fact, all the kids who were captivated by the movie and its touching story of an unlikely friendship between Elliot and E.T. tended to identify with the

Videogiochi #3, March 1983, pp. 63–65.

Trying to get out from a well for the *n*th time.

kid and not with the baby alien who they had to impersonate in the game! This design flaw may have affected subconsciously many young players, making it difficult for them to relive the excitement of the movie.

In the end, this is how things were envisioned by the designer, with the player hopefully immersed in the game and excited about escaping from the bad guys while searching for the three missing phone pieces. Unfortunately, as we saw, things turned out quite differently for a number of reasons, and this game is even considered by many as one of the causes of the infamous "videogame crash" in 1983 (see, for example, [Bogost and Montfort 09, page 76), when it seemed that people completely lost interest in videogames and many software and hardware companies had to file for bankruptcy. An alternative, and likely more appealing, design that might have partially saved the game commercially and somewhat limited its huge losses, should have probably been to base the game instead around the emotional scheme on the following page (see the second On the Way to Fun Diagram).

In this concept, kids would have had the opportunity to play as Elliot and help E.T. in his quest to go back home, maybe by indirectly controlling his movements ("herding" dynamic) to push him in safe places far from his enemies while also looking for the pieces of his phone.

E.T. the Extra-Terrestrial

E.T. the Extra-Terrestrial

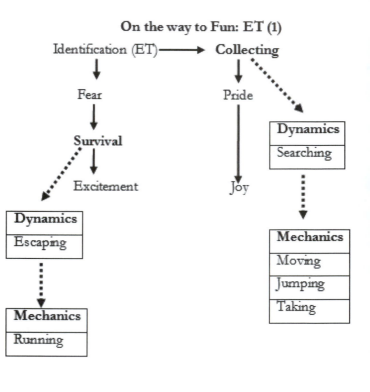

On the way to Fun: ET (1)

Identification (ET) ⟶ **Collecting**

Fear

Survival

Excitement

Dynamics
Escaping

Mechanics
Running

Pride

Joy

Dynamics
Searching

Mechanics
Moving
Jumping
Taking

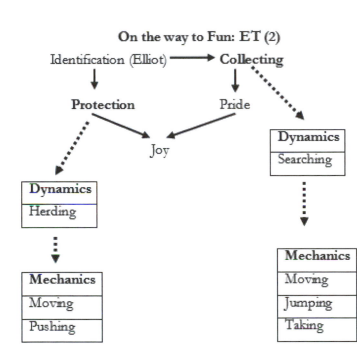

On the way to Fun: ET (2)

Identification (Elliot) ⟶ Collecting

Protection   Pride

Joy

Dynamics
Searching

Dynamics
Herding

Mechanics
Moving
Pushing

Mechanics
Moving
Jumping
Taking

E.T. the Extra-Terrestrial

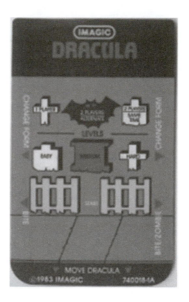

Intellivision controller overlay.

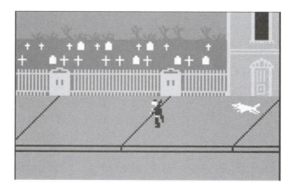

Intellivision controller overlay and in-game screenshot.
It's almost dawn and the Count is chased by a wolf!

Aesthetics	Dynamics	Mechanics	Other
aggressiveness	exploring	running	familiarity
color	chasing	flying	
appreciation	attacking	transforming	
curiosity	escaping	hiding	
familiarity		biting	
identification			
survival			

Making a game instantly familiar and recognizable may be easier than many people think if we can rely on a well-known character, for example one taken from hundred-year-old stories or well-known folklore. This was the case with Dracula, designed by Alan Smith on the Intellivision for Imagic in 1983. This game felt extremely exciting at the time, as it gave players the chance to play as one of the bad guys par excellence—the legendary lord vampire.

In this side-scrolling action game, the player had to mercilessly stalk his victims at night by roaming the silent streets of a colorfully portrayed city in a sort of two-and-a-half-dimensional representation while, at the same time, beware of the local constable and other enemies such as white wolves. To fight them, the player could turn his next victim into a zombie or transform himself into a bat and fly away, though vultures might be waiting for him in the sky. Moreover, before dawn (announced by a gradual change in the sky colors), he also had to go back to his "bedroom" (i.e., the local cemetery), as proper vampire traditions recommend.

The whole game experience was very carefully crafted, and it relied on a few different instincts to bring excitement to players, as we can see from the diagram. First, the graphics were quite detailed and colorful, making the player willing to roam around and explore the city while also helping in setting up the mood for a proper identification with the legendary character.

Dracula

This helped the player in "feeling" Dracula's powers but, at the same time, also made him aware of the city dangers and its pitfalls. Another big component in defining the overall emotional experience was aggressiveness, as the player would unleash it to chase any passer-by and then bite him to satisfy his thirst for blood as the real Dracula would have done.

This dynamic shows us an example of aggressiveness driven by the identification with the main character, and we should also point out that playing as a monster and killing innocent people was quite a bold and dangerous design choice at the time. Perhaps, also thanks to the lack of visible blood and to some humorous touches (e.g., to lure a possible victim, identified by a pair of eyes behind a window, out of their house by simply knocking at their door!), it didn't stir too many complaints and the game quickly became very popular among teenagers and young boys.

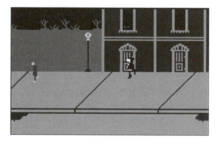

Knock-knock! "Who's there?" "It's Count Dracula. The night is still young, let's go out and have a drink!" "Yeah! You're right! I'm coming… AAHHHH!!!!"

Additionally, a strong competitive element was present, as two distinct two-player modes added another layer of fun and excitement to the overall experience. In addition to the standard mode where players would take turns to play as the vampire, there was also the option to play together, one player being Dracula and the other being the victim, switching roles each night.

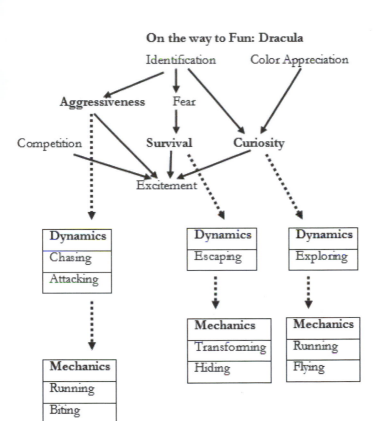

On the way to Fun: Dracula

Aesthetics	Dynamics	Mechanics
curiosity	exploring	talking
communication	conversing	moving
identification	information seeking	operating objects
protection/care	helping	
sadness	sharing experiences	

Since the early days of game development, game designers were fascinated with the idea of expanding their medium into new directions and delivering new experiences. Among those, a central idea emerged of telling more mature and complex stories that would immerse players so deeply as to make possible the emergence of different emotions, including those apparently unrelated to the concept of fun, such as sadness.

One of the first companies to make public such ambitious aims was Electronic Arts (EA) in what became one of the most famous ads in the history of video games.

Planetfall

Electronic Arts' famous ad published in 1982:
"Can a computer make you cry?"

Electronic Arts, though, wasn't the only company dreaming of elevating the video gaming genre to something more than a kid's pastime, as it was perceived by the general public; Infocom was another. Infocom was founded in 1979 by a group of enthusiast programmers from the Massachusetts Institute of Technology to develop text-based adventure games (a genre that is still surviving today in a niche called "interactive fiction") and from the very beginning, they showed they could deliver complex stories that were able to completely immerse players in fantastic virtual worlds. This achievement was even more valuable since it was obtained without relying on graphics or frantic joystick action but by stimulating players' fantasy instead, something they made sure to stress in their early advertising campaigns.

One of Infocom's original advertisements. "I know now there is more to life than joysticks," says the former "zombie," now back to life thanks to an Infocom game that talked to his imagination, waking him up (note the Atari 2600-like joystick).

Then, in 1983, one of Infocom's designers, Steve Meretzky, wrote *Planetfall*, a game that successfully answered EA's question. How did he achieve that? First, as we said, all Infocom games were extremely immersive. Although there were no graphics, the text parser was so good that communicating with the few NPCs, or even directly with the machine to interact with the environment, worked wonders in helping players identify with their character and get into the plot.

In this particular adventure, originally released for MS-DOS, TRS-80, TI 99/4A, Atari 8-bit, and Apple II, and later ported to Commodore 64 and other systems, one played as a guy who was onboard a spaceship that soon crashed on a deserted planet. Once there, the player meets a friendly and childlike robot named Floyd who'd join and help him throughout the quest of finding a way to go back home.

The interaction with Floyd was the key element of the whole game, as it provided humorous moments (like the robot yelling "Oh, boy! Are we going to try something dangerous?" when saving the game) while gradually setting a very strong bond between the player, the world, and the little robot. This bond was going to be ultimately broken towards the end of the game when Floyd sacrificed itself in saving the player. That was an emotionally intense moment that sincerely moved many players to tears, showing that games could really engage people very deeply and, ultimately, even make them cry.

Planetfall

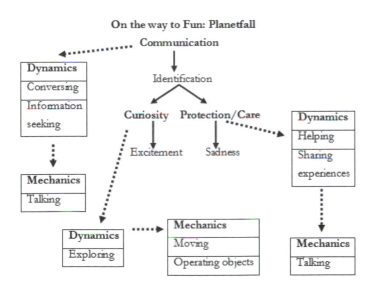

Safecracker

Aesthetics	Dynamics	Mechanics
collecting	exploring	driving
color appreciation	escaping	accelerating
curiosity	fighting	decelerating
fear	hacking	aiming
identification	searching	shooting
greed		operating
survival		taking
pride		

Programmed by Marvin Mednick and published by Imagic for the Intellivision in 1983, *Safecracker* put us into the shoes of a secret agent (a role that has always excited the fantasy of countless youngsters since the first James Bond 007 movies in the sixties) in a risky mission to retrieve sensitive documents and valuables from embassies of hostile countries. The game was worthy of attention for several reasons, as it combined different game dynamics and genres like driving, shooting, chasing, and simple puzzles. In doing so, it allowed players to freely roam a very detailed and colorful city, represented in isometric perspective, where he'd drive around in his blue car searching for the next embassy to target. Interestingly, the screen border colors were used as directional cues, as explained in the controller overlay. For example, a red border meant "go northwest" and a green

Safecracker

Driving and shooting in a trafficked city searching for secret documents.

one meant "go southeast." While this made the game even more colorful and visually appealing, it was also known to have confused some players who easily got lost in the city and who'd have preferred a traditional arrow or compass to point the way.

In *hard* mode the city presented some heavy traffic and, if the player collided with any car, the accident would make both vehicles explode. One could also shoot other cars and make them blow up, but this would attract the attention of the police who would start looking out for you, leading to exciting chases and shootouts.

Once the player reached the target embassy and parked nearby, he'd move into the simple puzzle section where he had to identify the safe combination within a small amount of time. If he were too slow, he could even decide to use harsh means and open it with some TNT, but this would also attract the police who would chase him as soon as he went back to his vehicle.

Trying to crack the combination. We need to go through all numbers carefully to identify the ones that "tick."

Overall, despite some relatively cumbersome controls, this game successfully relied on different instincts. To make the player willing to explore the city, color appreciation and curiosity were the starting points upon which the driving game, with its shootouts and chases, contributed to building pressure and excitement (thanks to the fight-or-flight survival response). At the same time, the simple combination-cracking mini-game added more variety to the overall experience by relating the action to the collection and greed instincts for grabbing new secrets and gold.

On the way to fun: Safecracker

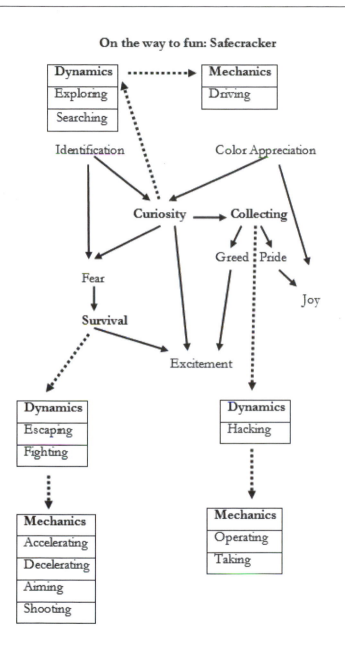

Seven Cities of Gold

1984, Electronic Arts

Aesthetics	Dynamics	Mechanics
aggressiveness	exploring	moving
curiosity	travelling	placing (buildings, units)
greed	conquering	killing
pride	trading	buying
		selling

Designed by Dani Bunten and originally released for the Atari 8-bit, Commodore 64, and Apple II, and later ported to the Amiga, PC, and Mac, *Seven Cities of Gold* was a groundbreaking adventure/strategic game that pushed the medium toward new directions. For example, it was for this game that the now very common word "edutainment" was used for the first time, precisely by Electronic Arts' founder Trip Hawkins while introducing this game to the press to underscore its attention to recreating an historical period and serve as a history teaching tool and not only a fun game.

The game is set in 1492 where we find ourselves in the shoes of a Spanish conquistador who has been appointed the mission of exploring the New World. Ultimately, aside from the curiosity for exploring an uncharted land, the game was based on the instincts of greed and pride as our aim was to retrieve as much treasure as possible so that the Queen of Spain would promote us to the highest grades.

To achieve this, we had to carefully plan where to build forts and missions and how to behave with the local populations. We could try to trade peacefully or to behave more aggressively, like the real conquistadors. This was also an innovative feature that led players to make some interesting moral choices and question

Seven Cities of Gold

their in-game actions and behavior. The game, though highly strategic in nature, also had some original arcade sequences that made the overall experience more varied and attractive.

An arcade sequence on the Apple II.

Discovering new lands on the Commodore 64.

On the way to fun: Seven Cities of Gold

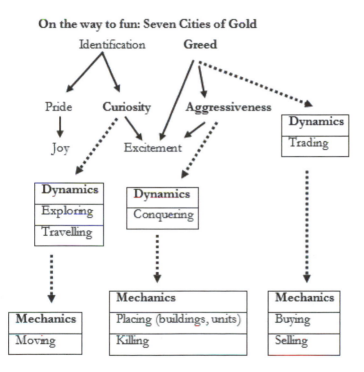

Spy vs. Spy

Aesthetics	Dynamics	Mechanics	Other
anger	exploring	moving	familiarity
competition	combining objects	taking	
curiosity	fighting	browsing	
identification		operating	
pride		stabbing	
revenge		placing (traps)	

Based on a comic strip made famous by the British magazine *MAD*, *Spy vs. Spy* was a very original action game for one or two players, released on different systems including the Apple II, Commodore 64, ZX Spectrum, Amstrad CPC, and later Amiga, Atari ST, and Sega Master System. The aim of the game was to retrieve a briefcase full of top-secret documents hidden in a big embassy and then to escape. Both players/spies had the same objective, so they had to defeat each other in any possible way first. To do so, they could fight each other directly if they met or, in a much more original and cunning way, they could experiment by collecting different objects and placing them to arrange deadly and sometimes funny traps to temporarily stop the other spy.

The gameplay was able to really excite players thanks to a very strong competitive setting while also stimulating their curiosity by pushing them to experiment with all possible objects and traps to see how they could stop the other spy, which was usually done through some funny and exhilarating animations. From a psychological perspective, placing a successful trap was also a very good way to make the scoring player feel smart and proud of his achievement, while making the other player angry and wishful for revenge.

Spy vs. Spy was also a notable and very original game from a technical viewpoint. In fact, it was one of the very first games to simulate a complete interaction with the environment (every

Spy vs. Spy

object displayed could have been used) while also featuring a split screen to let players play simultaneously but independently from each other.

Setting a trap on the Commodore 64.

The trap worked! The first spy laughs with satisfaction while the other is temporarily stunned and loses precious time (Amstrad CPC version).

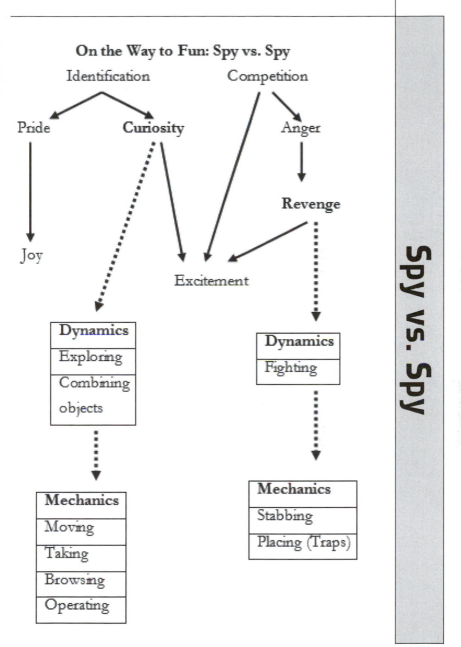

On the Way to Fun: Spy vs. Spy

Identification — Pride, Curiosity

Competition — Anger

Pride → Joy

Anger → Revenge

Curiosity → Excitement

Revenge → Excitement

Curiosity →

Dynamics
Exploring
Combining objects

→

Mechanics
Moving
Taking
Browsing
Operating

Revenge →

Dynamics
Fighting

→

Mechanics
Stabbing
Placing (Traps)

Spy vs. Spy

Little Computer People

1985, Activision

Aesthetics	Dynamics	Mechanics
communication	conversing	writing
protection/care	herding	reading
pride	helping	operating (objects)

Developed by David Crane and Sam Nelson for the Apple II, Commodore 64, Amstrad CPC, and later ported to the ZX Spectrum (128 k), Atari ST, and Amiga, *Little Computer People* was the game that started the "virtual life" genre that today includes very common household names like the *Sims* series and Tamagotchi. The game was all about a little guy and his dog living inside our computer and our task was to follow them during their daily life and to help whenever they needed our support.

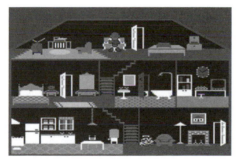

Practicing Beethoven's piano masterpieces in the attic while our dog rests downstairs waiting to be taken out for a jog (Commodore 64 screenshot).

The interaction with the virtual guy was simple but effective and fully rewarding. We could follow our little friend in all the rooms of his new house (except into the toilet), we could help him in keeping fit and in improving his musical skills, for example, and we could communicate with him to suggest many

Little Computer People

other activities (computer games included!) by typing simple commands. Once in a while he could also write us a letter providing valuable feedback about our actions so that we could know whether he was having a good life or, on the other hand, how we could improve things to make his life a little easier and more relaxing.

The possibility of communicating with the NPC by writing short messages and, in doing so, influencing his lifestyle, was the central idea upon which the whole gameplay was built. In fact, this bi-directional communication stream, where feedback was provided in the form of letters or by the performed actions themselves, really succeeded in making the player closer to the little guy supposedly living inside his computer. The resulting immersion was really very deep and players sincerely rejoiced by supervising the little guy's daily life as a sort of "guardian;" they felt proud for helping him in achieving his small daily successes and happiness. Graphics, animations, and sound effects were very cute in their simplicity and completed the overall charming picture, so it didn't take long for many players to perceive the little guy really like an old friend to take care of.

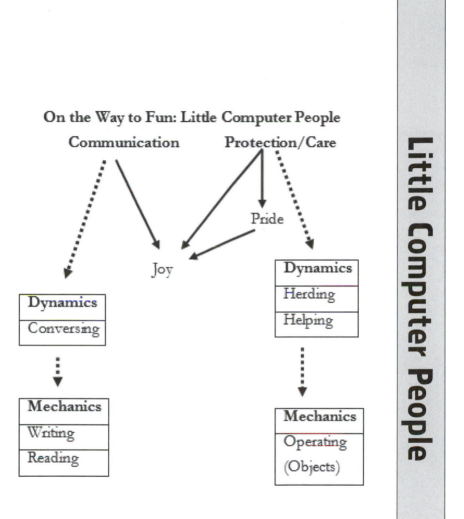

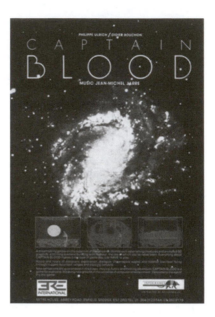

Original game advertisement.

Galaxy navigation screenshot (Amiga version).

Aesthetics	Dynamics	Mechanics
communication	exploring	point to point
curiosity	conversing	movement
identification	information seeking	accelerating
		decelerating
		talking

Developed by ERE Informatique and published by Infogrames on 8- and 16-bits systems (Commodore 64, ZX Spectrum, Amstrad CPC, Amiga, and Atari ST), this game presented itself with the fascinating slogan "Welcome to the age of the bio game," meaning that the NPCs were able to carry on their lives independent of the player's own actions. Undoubtedly, this very original sci-fi adventure promised, and delivered, a very immersive experience, even though its learning curve wasn't exactly smooth.

The starting premise was quite original, despite making some clear references to movies like *Tron* and other science-fiction themes. In this game, the player took the role of an unlucky programmer who got cloned and trapped in his own space game. Now he had to quickly find all his other five "selves" and kill them to avoid being mutated into a robot forever. Despite its slight weirdness, this premise successfully provided a captivating backdrop for the action and gave a sense of urgency related to the player's own survival. These elements, together with beautiful and colorful graphics, music, and an effective first-person view (the hyperspace sequence was considered memorable), contributed to immerse many players in the game and make them identify with Captain Blood, the game's main character.

Regarding the actual gameplay, the five clones were hiding somewhere on different systems of a huge galaxy that the player had to carefully explore looking for clues. The clues could be obtained by properly communicating with the many different alien creatures the player met in his explorations. Some were

Captain Blood

friendly, while others naturally were more aggressive but, no matter how nice or mean they looked and behaved towards the player, all of them could have some important information and it was up to the player to find a way to communicate properly with them, gain their trust, and ultimately find their clones.

This is where the game got truly original and fascinating, completely relying on our communication instinct to go through the seemingly impossible task of starting a dialogue with someone who didn't speak our language at all! To solve this problem, communication with aliens occurred via an icon-based interface (named UPCOM) consisting of about 150 icons, each representing a different concept. We had then to learn how to negotiate using those concepts in a style suitable to the different races, all of them having different personalities and needs— a truly fascinating approach that made this game unique and worth exploring.

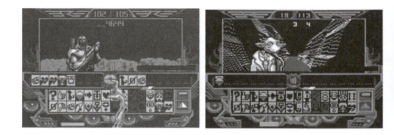

Different aliens, different personalities, and . . . different languages! How to communicate? By using the UPCOM of course! (Atari ST, left, and Commodore 64, right, screenshots.)

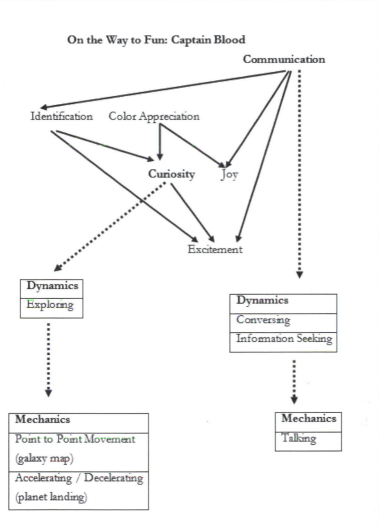

On the Way to Fun: Captain Blood

PART III

Case Studies: Indie Games

Why Indie Games?

More than twenty years have passed since the games discussed in Part II were released. During this time, the gaming industry has developed very fast and, most importantly, expanded in a variety of different directions. One of the most exciting areas to get the spotlight during the last few years has been the so-called "indie" scene where individual programmers, or very small teams, succeeded in experimenting with innovative concepts and ideas without all the constraints and worries typical of bigger developers.

Interestingly, indie developers are, in many cases, old enough to have started playing games in the eighties while often also taking part in development communities like the "demo-scenes"* of early home computers such as the Commodore 64. Being aware of such backgrounds can surely help us today in understanding their modern creations better and, by viewing their games in this light, it is easier to appreciate them also as a direct evolution of those early productions in several respects.

For example, modern indie games tend to be quite meaningful and ambitious in concept, constantly trying to break new ground despite being often constrained by few resources. This resembles very closely the working environment and aspirations of the old games, which were necessarily "original" since there was nothing before them and also had to be developed by taking into account the strict hardware limitations of the time. At the same time, indie developers showcase an unconditional love for the videogame medium as a form of self-expression and art, which transpires from the focus on gameplay mechanics and resulting aesthetics—exactly like the early pioneers did. This passion is

*See http://en.wikipedia.org/wiki/Demoscene for more information.

clearly a much stronger driving force than simply the desire to showcase the latest technologies and make money, which do not necessarily play a main role here.

But are the underlying emotions and instincts relevant in this new breed of games still the same as they were years ago? To try to answer this question, let's analyze a few of the most representative indie games as of 2009 and see what type of On the Way to Fun diagrams we get.

Toribash

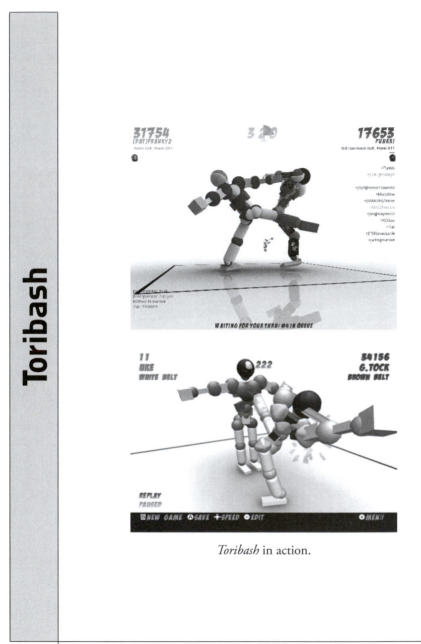

Toribash in action.

2006, Nabi Studios

Aesthetics	Dynamics	Mechanics
aggressiveness	customization	acquiring items
competition	attacking	user-generated content
communication	defending	punching
identification	dismembering	kicking
revenge	expressing	blocking
	showing off	sequencing
	sharing	conversing

Designed by Hampus Söderström, *Toribash* is an on-line turn-based fighting game using ragdoll physics available on PC, Mac, and the Nintendo Wii. The game was an Independent Game Festival finalist in 2007. The originality of this game lies in the possibility of planning for every joint movement of our fighter and preparing our strikes in any way we like, with effects that can literally dismember the other character.

Toribash

Showing off a newly-designed pair of pants and helmet for our ragdoll fighter.

As a multiplayer fighting game, aggressiveness and competition are obviously at the core of the emotional experience and can enhance each other, as indicated by the bi-directional arrow in the diagram. The clever evolution of the game throughout the last few years successfully expanded it into new directions, thanks to a very active and enthusiast user community. For example, a broad range of customization options grants a strong identification between the player and his ragdoll. This can even support other non-trivial aspects such as communication, by letting players express their own personal style and tastes in addition to clearly providing the chance of showing off in the community and, of course, giving even more topics to chat about in the forums and chat rooms.

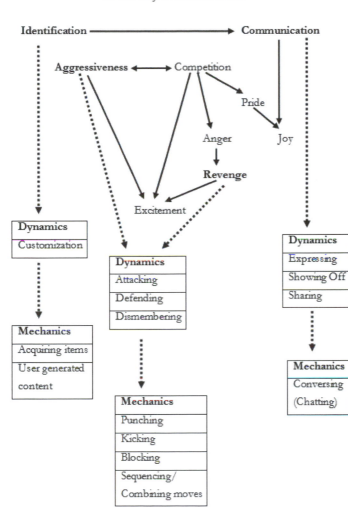

On the Way to Fun: Toribash

Braid

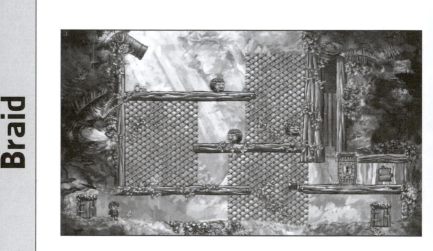

Braid—an emotionally charged platformer full of surprises.

Aesthetics	Dynamics	Mechanics
curiosity	exploring	running
identification	information seeking	jumping
sadness	reaching	climbing
color appreciation	unlocking	taking
		reading
	time manipulation	

Designed by Jonathan Blow and made public with instant critical acclaim by winning the Independent Game Festival in 2006, *Braid* was officially released on Xbox 360 as a downloadable game through Xbox Live Arcade (XBLA) in 2007 and later ported to PC, Mac, and PS3, *Braid* was, and still is, a very original and ambitious game where, under the hood of a normal-looking platformer (references to *Super Mario Bros.* and *Donkey Kong* abound), the playing experience is actually driven by a very original game mechanic consisting of manipulating time in various ways to solve complex puzzles.

The time-control feature allows players to learn from their own mistakes, making it possible to die without worries. Actually, dying even becomes an important aspect of the game as players start feeling free to explore different possibilities and strategies, getting more and more curious as the game progresses. Thanks to this new attitude they can really use all of their imagination to find creative solutions to successfully collect the different jigsaw pieces required and, ultimately, advance in the game. This innovative concept, together with very charming graphics and music tied to a complex storyline built around a lost love which we discover little by little by reading different panels, completely immersed countless players into the game and made *Braid* an instant classic and one of the most well-known indie games ever.

Braid

In analyzing the game, it is interesting to note how the ability to juggle between the in-game's simple successes (like collecting a puzzle piece) and the seriousness of the story line allowed *Braid* to provoke contrasting emotions in its players, ranging from joy and happiness to sadness, including corresponding variants such as disappointment and satisfaction. In addition, in *Braid* we also see how color appreciation can play an important role in determining the final appeal of a modern indie game, as *Braid* was also widely prized for its quality artwork.

At first, this may seem in contradiction to our original statement that "gameplay is king" and that graphics are not as relevant. Nonetheless, if we look a little deeper, we can easily understand that, in this context, "graphics" doesn't mean relying on the computer's computational power but, on the contrary, its aim is to capture the player's attention and imagination by artistic means. Once this is achieved, it will be up to the other gameplay dynamics to successfully immerse the player in the action by exploiting other instincts and emotions (for example, through the curiosity instinct towards exploration and by collecting specific items to get deeper into the story)—something that *Braid* did masterfully.

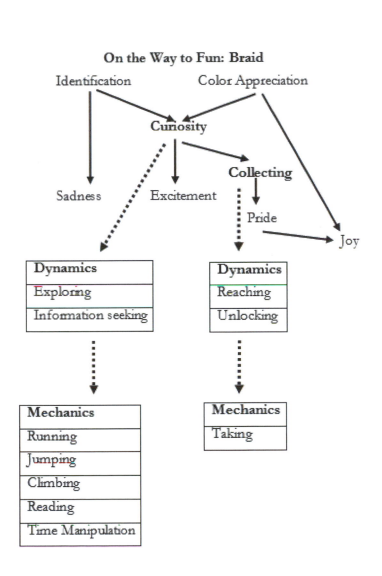

On the Way to Fun: Braid

Identification   Color Appreciation

Curiosity

Sadness   Excitement   Collecting

Pride

Joy

Dynamics
Exploring
Information seeking

Dynamics
Reaching
Unlocking

Mechanics
Running
Jumping
Climbing
Reading
Time Manipulation

Mechanics
Taking

Braid

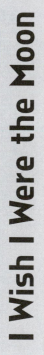

I Wish I Were the Moon

A boy, a girl, and the Moon form an odd but amusing love-triangle game with multiple endings.

2008, Daniel Benmergui

Aesthetics	Dynamics	Mechanics
collecting	helping	taking snapshots
curiosity	storytelling	arranging
pride		
protection		
sadness		

Inspired by the novel *The Distance of the Moon* from the *Cosmicomiche* by Italian writer Italo Calvino, *I Wish I Were the Moon** is a little work of art that defies classifications. It is the game that brought its author, Daniel Benmergui, to international attention thanks to its appearances at the Sense of Wonder Night (Tokyo Game Show, 2008) and at the Experimental Gameplay Workshop (Game Developers Conference in San Francisco, 2009).

Here there is no score, which means no competition, and no enemies to defeat. Instead, we are simply given a canvas on which we can play out different storylines by taking snapshots of parts of the screen (displayed in beautiful retro-styled graphics) and move them around to see what happens. This simple mechanic lets us interact with different characters, setting up a bond that will soon start to make us care for the boy and girl NPCs in the game and eager to see how we can manipulate the environment to make them happy or, failing to do so, sad and even desperate. Disaster endings are also included, which can make us feel really surprised at first and then very sad and willing to try again to find another happier ending.

As we can see, there are two main starting instincts that work in parallel to immerse players into the virtual setting— protecting and helping the NPCs to be happy kicks in early in the game, bringing different emotions according to the particular ending. At the same time, the search for the ending is

I Wish I Were the Moon

*The game is freely playable from Benmergui's website: http://www.ludomancy.com/blog/2008/09/03/i-wish-i-were-the-moon/.

constantly motivated by the curiosity to experiment with the available objects and, ultimately, to find and collect all possible story variations. Most importantly, both instincts are stimulated by using the same in-game mechanics; i.e., by arranging the different objects and characters on-screen in different areas by using a simple camera snapshot procedure, showing that the same game elements can be used for different purposes.

Studying the On the Way to Fun diagram for this game is extremely interesting as it shows how even a game that seems very simple on its surface can instead hide a lot of thought and imaginative work.

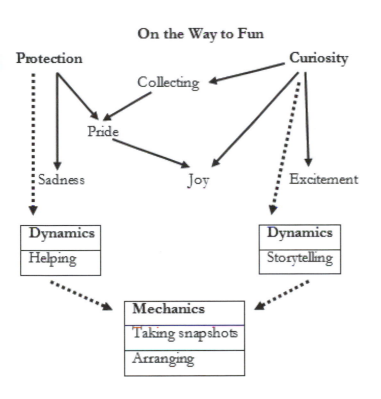

We will have to save not one but four princesses here!
Let the adventure begin!

Aesthetics	Dynamics	Mechanics
aggressiveness	exploring	moving
collecting	experimenting	jumping
competition	helping each other	choosing a path
curiosity	leveling up	riding
greed	winning (prizes)	browsing (items)
identification	acquiring (objects,	joining forces
protection	bonuses)	distributing (skill
	fighting	points)
	conquering	buying
	crashing	taking (gold, objects)
		striking
		breaking
		using magic
		powering

Castle Crashers

Released first on Xbox 360 and then also on the PlayStation 3 (PS3) as a downloadable title, *Castle Crashers* is a direct descendent of the side scrolling "beat-em-up" games that were so popular in the arcades twenty years ago. Being a "beat-em-up" game, aggressiveness clearly plays a fundamental role here from the very beginning of the gaming experience. In *Castle Crashers* though, it is never portrayed seriously and it is instead cleverly conveyed into an exhilarating gameplay frenzy by characters that are cute and easy to identify with. A multiplayer cooperative (co-op) mode also adds a lot of fun to the action by offering to four players an uncommon protection element consisting of the possibility of helping each other when in need.

The protection theme doesn't stop there, though, and it is always present in the background, as often happens in these kinds of games. This time we have to rescue not only one, but as many as four, unlucky princesses (one for each valiant knight/ player?) who have been kidnapped by an evil wizard and hidden away somewhere in a fairy-tale medieval land full of secrets to uncover and enemies to defeat. Other elements are also added to the final mix. In fact, with plenty of power-ups to collect and gold to pick up and use to buy new add-ons and goodies, there are many ways to keep players interested and to let them prove who is the most powerful and brave knight in the land.

On the Way to Fun: Castle Crashers

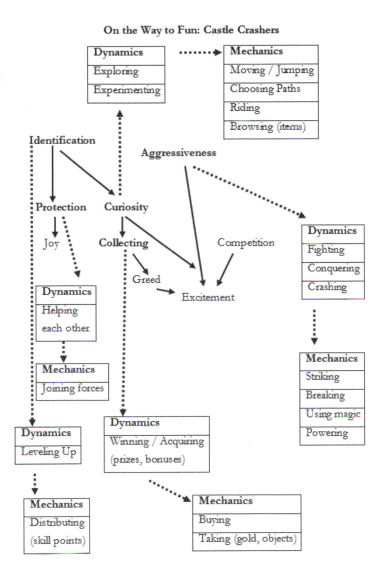

Tag

Tag—painting the city has never been so much fun!

Aesthetics	Dynamics	Mechanics
color appreciation	exploring	moving
curiosity	painting	accelerating
identification		jumping
pride		sticking
		spraying
		cleaning
		choosing (colors)

Developed by seven students from the DigiPen Institute of Technology and winner of the Independent Games Festival (IGF) 2009 Best Student Game Award, *Tag: The Power of Paint** is a very original first-person puzzle/platformer where colors play the main role across the whole gaming experience. All puzzles have to be solved by spraying different varnishes on a completely grey cityscape. Each color will grant the player a special ability or power-up to overcome a specific obstacle. For example, spraying red in front of the player and then walking over it will allow him to run faster; green will allow him to jump, and so on.

These game mechanics are clearly designed to strongly resonate with our color appreciation instinct while also encouraging players to experiment in different ways across the city areas. This turns out to be an important part of the game, not only to solve the cleverly designed puzzles and reach the end of the level, but also to simply have fun by restoring lively colors to the environment, bringing both joy and excitement at the same time.

In its simplicity and originality, *Tag* shows us that color appreciation is a very powerful instinct that can be evoked not only through beautiful and artistic graphics (as in other games such as *Braid*) but also by a simple and neat graphical style where there is almost no color to start with! The absence of colors will then act like a trigger to make us notice how much more beautiful things would be if properly painted. All of the remaining

*More information on the game, its developers, and a download link can be found at https://www.digipen.edu/studentprojects/tag/.

parts of the game will then allow us to satisfy our subconscious thirst for colors by providing a good excuse to paint the city anew and, in doing so, it will also successfully deliver an immersive and fun experience.

On the Way to Fun: TAG

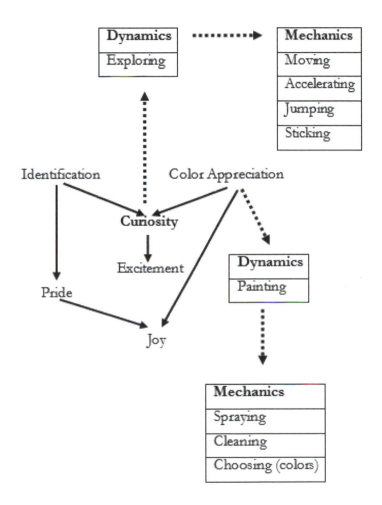

Flower

Gently blowing on a flower.

2009, Thatgamecompany

Aesthetics	Dynamics	Mechanics
collecting	exploring	flying
color appreciation	searching	touching
curiosity	herding	grouping
identification		guiding
pride		
protection		

Released exclusively on the PlayStation 3 as a downloadable game, Flower quickly established itself as one of the most inspired and successful productions on the PlayStation Network (PSN). Designed by Jenova Chen, this game succeeds in immersing players in a new, yet familiar, experience. By taking the role of the wind, the player has to freely roam across different countryside scenarios and landscapes. These are all beautifully drawn, and while the player roams the objective is to gather and guide together a growing group of petals with the ultimate goal of making nature blossom again.

The whole game stresses the search for emotions related to joy and freedom, inviting players to be curious and explore what lies behind the next boundary, such as a hill or, like at the very start of the game, a grey, polluted, and sad cityscape. An effective first-person view, intuitive controls, and inspired music work in synergy to create a great resulting mix, fully immersing the player in the game's virtual nature and making him one with the blowing wind. The interaction with the petals, on the other hand, also works perfectly to make them feel alive and something the player wants to care about and nurture throughout his journey.

Flower

Flower

This is also effectively used to induce a protection instinct toward the petals, which is then expressed and fulfilled by a herding dynamic thanks to the possibility of grouping them together and having them follow us throughout the levels.

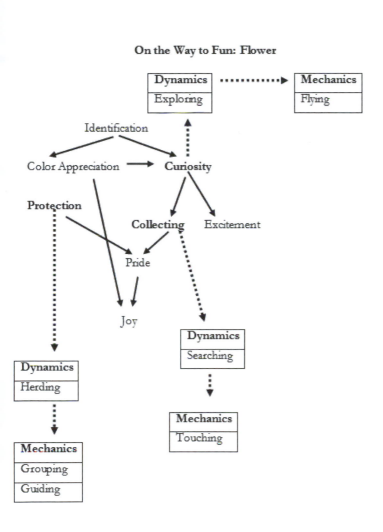

On the Way to Fun: Flower

Flower

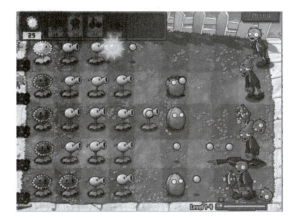

Getting ready for the final-level assault.

Aesthetics	Dynamics	Mechanics
curiosity	defending	placing
collecting	acquiring (new plants)	removing
fear	storing (energy)	choosing
identification		taking
survival		
pride		

"Tower defense" games are not new (the first example dates back as early as 1990 with Atari's arcade game *Rampart*) but they became very popular only in recent times with *Plants vs. Zombies* being one of the latest and most successful examples.

This downloadable game, designed by George Fan and published by PopCap on PC, Mac, and Xbox 360, sounds as unlikely and crazy as it is fun. The cute graphics play a pivotal role in setting up a cheerful mood from the very beginning, and the player is smoothly introduced to the game's mechanics by the first tutorial levels, making a classical "help" section superfluous. Nonetheless, there still is a little "help" window, which tells you "[w]hen the zombies show up, just sit there and don't do anything. You win the game when the zombies get to your houze —this help section brought to you by the Zombies." This kind of humor pervades the whole playing experience.

Identification is sought after from the very beginning too. The player is asked for his or her own name before the game starts, and then the first thing we see is our own house under attack by the first waves of zombies! Even though the tone of the game is clearly humorous, having hordes of zombies walking relentlessly toward a player's house to eat his brains is surely liable to excite some fear in the heart of most players, bringing in the survival instinct and the wish to fight back through our green

Plants vs. Zombies

allies. Because escaping is not an option as we are under siege, the game is instantly involving. With 49 different types of plants, power-ups, 26 types of zombies, and 50 levels, there is a lot to be curious about and plenty of items to collect, providing a long lasting interest in the game.

Plants vs. Zombies

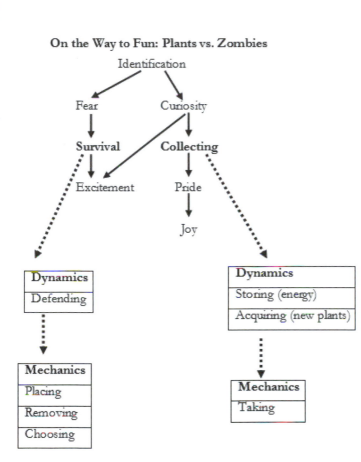

On the Way to Fun: Plants vs. Zombies

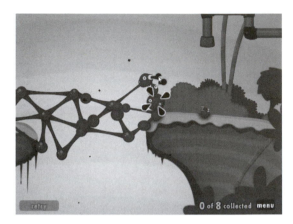

An early level in *World of Goo*.

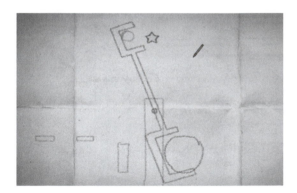

Crayon Physics Deluxe.

Aesthetics	Dynamics	Mechanics
collecting	interacting	building
curiosity	herding	dragging (WoGoo)
pride	reaching	drawing
		pushing (CPDL)

World of Goo & Crayon Physics Deluxe

For our last case study, let's have a look at a very popular genre of indie games—physics-based puzzles. In this group, the two most well-known games released lately were *World of Goo*, designed by Kyle Gabler of 2D Boy and winner of the Design Innovation and Technical Excellence awards at the IGF Festival 2008 (available on PC, Mac, and Wii) and *Crayon Physics Deluxe* by Petri Purho of Kloonigames, Grand Prize Winner at the IGF Festival 2008 (released on PC only so far).

These games make strong use of physics to simulate a world that, despite its fantasy traits, feels and behaves as naturally as we would expect from our everyday life and experience. Most important, it is a world that players are completely free to analyze and interact with in order to study its reactions and then solve its increasingly difficult puzzles.

As shown in the figure, the curiosity to interact realistically with the objects and constraints of the virtual world by building new "goo-made" structures or objects by simply drawing them is the key to captivating players' attention. Once this is achieved, the gameplay focuses on the collection instinct to keep players motivated. In both games, we have to indirectly control something, known as the herding dynamic. In *Crayon Physics* we have to push a ball toward a shiny star, while in *World of Goo* we have to bring our cute balls of goo next to the exit of that game level to be properly collected. Both games are very successful in their endeavors, and passing each level—whether by reaching the little star or by pushing the last dark goo ball into a jar—feels very satisfying and rewarding.

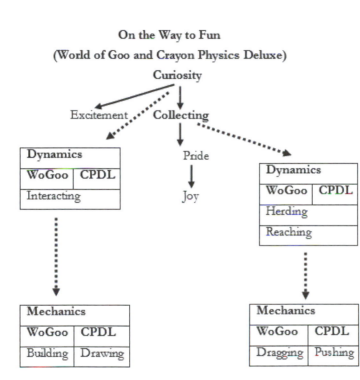

On the Way to Fun
(World of Goo and Crayon Physics Deluxe)

PART IV

Conclusions

In the End

Our various examples should have illustrated how basic emotions and instincts, as exemplified by the 6-11 Framework, were used to shape the aesthetics of old games and also how they were reinterpreted in new, innovative indie productions. So, what kinds of common traits or general rules can we extrapolate from these analyses? Is there a recipe for making fun and engaging games? Well, obviously a perfect recipe doesn't exist because the final result is determined by all of the countless factors—and almost infinite combinations of them—that define the game design in all its different nuances. However, we can hopefully still identify some particular ingredients that are more likely than others to add some "spicy" flavors to our final dish.

To start with, we saw that most games have as their first important objective the task of making the player feel like one with his or her in-game character. We can conclude that the identification instinct is usually one of the first that needs to be incorporated. This can be achieved in several ways, including

- first-person perspective (e.g., *Battlezone* or *Flower*),
- extensive customization options (e.g., *Toribash*),
- an engaging story (e.g., *Planetfall* or *Braid*).

Once the identification has been accomplished, a mix of different instincts to motivate the player is needed. In Part I we divided our 11 main instincts into three groups: first person, third person, and world, each of which can be used to engage the player in different ways. Usually, for games based mostly on a single-player action, world related instincts, like curiosity and color appreciation can appear first and then act as a link toward other instincts in the first-person group like collecting and greed which, in turn, can lead to aggressiveness or revenge in the third-person category. On the other hand, in games focused on multiplayer the third-person instinct of competition is often one of the most relevant. It can emerge early and be very powerful, especially in those cases where players have to face each other directly or indirectly to achieve the same or a similar objective. In this case, competition will be a leading component in influencing the subsequent emotional development of the playing experience, as in *Toribash*. In most cases, these instincts provide players with enough motivation to go through all the in-game challenges and hurdles that are thrown at them, resulting in the emergence of different emotions like pride, anger, joy, and, as seen in some special cases, sadness. While instincts can provide a very general guideline regarding the aesthetics upon which to base our game design, what about the technical aspects?

Certainly, impressive graphics, animations, and sound do play an important role in the overall experience and can greatly help in attracting players, immersing them in the gaming world, and in increasing the overall appeal and fun-factor of a game. This, though, as exemplified by games such as *Braid* or *Flower*, should be seen more as a requirement needed from an artistic perspective where the graphics and soundscapes are functional in enhancing the aesthetics that characterize the gameplay's unique focus, and not as a mere tool to showcase technical and computational power.

We should also emphasize that, even though we just began these final comments by saying that identification is a likely starting point, we can easily also provide examples of how a beautiful and engaging game can be achieved without the need of having any identification at all! How this can be done will appear evident by looking back at games like *Little Computer People* or more recent examples like *Crayon Physics* Deluxe or

World of Goo. This apparent contradiction needn't be confusing. On the contrary, it should make us even more excited and willing to experiment further with our design ideas as it shows something of the videogame medium which is one of the true traits of any real art form—whatever rules we may find and think of, there will always be clever ways of breaking them and still achieve beautiful results.

And What About Other Games?

Now that we have an idea of the main criteria that can be used to design engaging experiences in simple and old-style games or recent indie productions, we may wonder whether the same approach can be used to get insights into modern "big" games as well. Clearly, so-called AAA titles can be way more complex, both technically and conceptually, than those analyzed in these pages, resulting in potentially far more articulated ways to fun. But generally speaking, we can still say that an immersive gaming experience should probably start by relying on an instinct, such as identification, to aim at emotions like excitement and joy. And we've pointed out that exceptions to the general principals are possible, too. Thanks to the huge technical advances allowing visionary game designers to shape new gameplay dynamics and experiences, we can have innovative games able to exploit specific basic emotions to allow players to feel even more subtle and complex ones. For example, in the critically acclaimed and painfully beautiful *Shadow of the Colossus*, designed by Fumito Ueda (2005, Sony Computer Entertainment for PS2), the player had to travel vast, deserted lands in a quest to fight and kill some apparently peaceful monsters. The game had no joy at all, and the excitement for a battle quickly faded into a very interesting elaboration on the emotion of sadness, specifically evoking loneliness and guilt.

In other examples, we can see how, even on the latest platforms, simple emotional schemes are still at the foundation of a beautiful and even innovative experience, as in ambitious, casual titles such as *Afrika* (2009, Natsume, Sony Computer Entertainment, PS3) or *Endless Ocean* (2008, Arika, Nintendo Wii) where color appreciation and curiosity for exploring the natural environments are the channels to bring excitement and joy to players.

Further examples of an emotional scheme with little or no identification can be found also in other very successful games, like most of those in the so-called *Match 3* casual games genre. In these games, excitement and joy are generated through color appreciation for objects to be matched, the curiosity to see the next level, collecting new items by matching them, the constant sense of progress from matching objects and seeing them disappear.

Analyzing finished games to understand their aesthetics and learn about their inner emotional structure, though, is not the only domain where our framework can be applied. In fact, and most important, it can also be used during the design process of a new game idea to ascertain whether the gameplay we are envisioning actually makes sense from a psychological perspective and can lead to the right set of aesthetics. If we can use our framework to properly trace the progress and development of the gaming experience through different emotions and instincts, our game will be more likely to resonate naturally with players at a subconscious level and engage them to the fullest. For example, we could decide to start designing a game from its aesthetics, by drafting a possible On the Way To Fun scheme. One way to do so would be to plan to use diversified instincts from all three groups (first person, third person, and world) and related emotions, creating a sort of emotional map that we can later fol-

On the way to Fun: Afrika, Endless Ocean

Identification   Color Appreciation

Curiosity

Excitement   Joy

Sample screenshots from *Afrika* for Sony PS3 (top) and *Endless Ocean* for Nintendo Wii (middle), and a possible On the Way to Fun emotional scheme to describe how they engage and immerse players (bottom).

Shadow of the Colossus.
We will find no joy here: only loneliness and guilt.

low by developing proper game dynamics and their underlying mechanics.

In this way, we are actually integrating our model in a design process that follows the MDA framework. Whether we decide to start our work from the mechanics (i.e., game rules), proceed to the dynamics, and then to the subsequent aesthetics as identified by the On the Way To Fun diagram or choose to work the other way round, using the 6-11 Framework as a starting point to plan for the aesthetics, develop the required dynamics, and finally craft the mechanics accordingly, we are actually progressing in a structured and sound way that will keep the whole design process focused and on track with the original vision, significantly increasing our chances of success.

On the way to Fun: 7 Wonders

Color Appreciation

Curiosity

Collecting

Pride ⟶ Joy

Excitement

Screenshot from *Cradle of Rome* (2008, Cerasus Media, D3Publisher, Nintendo DS) (top), one of the latest *Match 3* games (middle), and its corresponding emotional scheme (bottom).

References

[Montfort and Bogost 09] Nick Montfort and Ian Bogost. *Racing the Beam: The Atari Video Computer System*. Cambridge, MA: MIT Press, 2009.

[Brathwaite and Schreiber 08] Brenda Brathwaite and Ian Schreiber. *Challenges for Game Designers*. Boston: Charles River Media, 2008.

[Crawford 84] Chris Crawford. *The Art of Computer Game Design*. Berkeley, CA: McGraw-Hill Osborne Media, 1984.

[Ekman 99] Paul Ekman. "Basic Emotions." In *Handbook of Cognition and Emotion*, edited by Tim Dalgleish and Mick Power. Sussex, UK: John Wiley & Sons, Ltd., 1999.

[Ekman 04] Paul Ekman. *Emotions Revealed: Recognizing Faces and Feelings to Improve Communication and Emotional Life*. New York: Henry Holt and Company, LLC, 2004.

[Freeman 04] David Freeman. *Creating Emotions in Games: The Craft and Art of Emotioneering*. Berkeley, CA: New Riders Publishing, 2004.

[Hunicke et al 04] Robin Hunicke, Marc LeBlanc, and Robert Zubek. *MDA: A Formal Approach to Game Design and Game Research*. Prepared for Proceedings of the Challenges in Game AI Workshop, Nineteenth National Conference on Artificial Intelligence, San Jose, CA, July 25–29, 2004.

[Isbister 06] Katherine Isbister. *Better Game Characters by Design: A Psychological Approach*. San Francisco: Morgan Kaufmann Publishers, 2006.

[Izard 77] Carroll E. Izard. *Human Emotions*. New York: Plenum Press, 1977.

[Lazzaro 09] Nicole Lazzaro. "Understand Emotions." In *Beyond Game Design: Nine Steps Toward Creating Better Videogames*, edited by Chris Bateman. Boston: Charles River Media, 2009.

[Plutchik 80] Robert Plutchik. "A General Psychoevolutionary Theory of Emotion." In *Emotion. Theory, Research, and Experience: Volume 1: Theories of Emotion*, edited by Robert Plutchik and Henry Hellerman, pp. 3–33. New York: Academic Press, 1980.

[Robertson, 1987] I. Robertson: *Sociology: An Introduction*. New York: Worth Publishers, 1987.

[Weiner and Graham, 1984] B. Weiner, S. Graham: "An Attributional Approach to Emotional Development." In *Emotions, Cognition, and Behavior*, edited by Carroll E. Izard, Jerome Kagan, and Robert B. Zajonc, pp. 167–191. Cambridge UK: Cambridge University Press 1984.

Index

E

eating. See taking

escaping 9, 29, 41, 49, 50, 57, 65, 73, 76, 79, 83, 85, 89, 97

excitement 8, 14, 16, 19, 27, 28, 49, 54, 57, 66, 70, 80, 85, 89, 90, 98, 139, 159, 160

experimenting 135

exploring 13, 57, 69, 73, 79, 89, 93, 97, 101, 105, 113, 114, 127, 135, 139, 143, 160

expressing 123

F

familiarity 23, 27, 37, 53, 57, 61, 69, 73, 79, 83, 89, 105

fear 5, 7, 15, 45, 57, 73, 74, 76, 79, 80, 97, 147

fighting 29, 37, 45, 65, 73, 97, 105, 123, 135

flying 89, 143

G

greed 10, 14, 18, 73, 76, 97, 98, 101, 135, 158

grouping 143

guiding 143

H

hacking 97

happiness. See joy

helping 10, 93, 109, 110, 131, 135

helping each other 135

herding 83, 85, 109, 143, 151

hiding 37, 89

I

identification 9, 13, 19, 20, 21, 27, 28, 45, 46, 53, 65, 69, 73, 79, 83, 84, 89, 93, 97, 105, 113, 123, 124, 127, 135, 139, 143, 147, 157, 158, 159

immediateness 23, 37, 38

information seeking 93, 113, 127

interacting 151

J

joining forces 135

joy 7, 15, 19, 27, 28, 57, 61, 65, 128, 139, 143, 158, 159, 160, 162

jumping 41, 60, 69, 83, 127, 135, 139

K

kicking 123

killing 101

About the Author

Roberto Dillon was born in Genoa, Italy, in 1973. He holds a Master's and a PhD in Electrical and Computer Engineering from the University of Genoa. His research focuses on analyzing emotions within interactive multimedia applications. His projects include *M-EDGE: The Music and Emotion Driven Game Engine*, a technology that combines expression of emotion with real-time musical instruments, and *Virtual Orchestra*, a children's game that USA Today called "Guitar Hero for the symphony crowd."

He tecahes at the Singapore campus of the DigiPen Institute of Technology where he is an assistant professor in Game Design and Real Time Interactive Simulations.

You can reach him at http://www.ProgramAndPlay.com.